A Time to Say Good-Bye

Moving Beyond Loss

To Ila
with all best wishes
Mary Goulding

Also by Mary McClure Goulding:

Sweet Love Remembered

Books by
Mary McClure Goulding and Robert L. Goulding:

Changing Lives Through Redecision Therapy
The Power Is in the Patient
Not to Worry

A Time to Say Good-Bye

Moving Beyond Loss

Mary McClure Goulding, MSW

Papier-Mache Press
Watsonville CA

00 99 98 97 96 5 4 3 2 1

ISBN: 0-918949-74-2 Softcover

Copyediting by *Janet Ring*

Cover photograph by *David Bracher*

Cover design by *Cynthia Heier*

Interior design and text composition by *Leslie Austin* and *Erin Lebacqz*

Proofreading by *Erin Lebacqz*

Manufactured by *Malloy Lithographing, Inc.*

Grateful acknowledgment is made to the following publications which first published some of the material in this book:

The chapter titled "Death" is reprinted from *Sweet Love Remembered* (TA Press, 1992), a biography of Robert L. Goulding, by Mary McClure Goulding. Excerpt from "Departure" by Edna St. Vincent Millay. From *Collected Poems*, HarperCollins. © 1923, 1951 by Edna St. Vincent Millay and Norma Millay Ellis. Reprinted by permission of Elizabeth Barnett, literary executor.

Library of Congress Cataloging-in-Publication Data
Goulding, Mary McClure, 1925–
Time to say good-bye: moving beyond loss / Mary Goulding.
p. cm.
ISBN 0-918949-75-0 (alk. paper). — ISBN 0-918949-74-2 (pbk.: alk. paper)
1. Goulding, Mary McClure, 1925–. 2. Widows—United States—Biography. 3. Widowhood—United States—Psychological aspects—Case studies. 4. Bereavement in old age—United States—Case studies. 5. Loss (Psychology) in old age—United States—Case studies. 6. Psychotherapists—United States—Biography. I. Title.
HQ1058.5.U5G68 1996
305.48'9654'092—dc20
[B] 95-26563
CIP

This book is printed on acid-free, recycled paper containing a minimum of 85 percent total recycled fiber with 15 percent postconsumer de-inked fiber.

to the memory of
Bob Goulding

Contents

A Time to Say Good-Bye

Moving Beyond Loss

Greater than gods are we who dare to love
While sentenced to mortality.
—Peter Viereck, "The Eagle"

Introduction

As a child I was fascinated and frightened whenever I glimpsed white-haired, old ladies alone in their homes. I'd see them in their apartments in Chicago, sitting at their windows behind bright red, potted geraniums. As I roller-skated on the sidewalks of the suburb where I lived, I'd glimpse them through their windows, moving slowly from room to room, more like trembling reflections than living women. They all looked alike, slightly bent, dressed darkly, with wispy white hair that stood up from their heads.

I was certain they never went outside, but remained forever behind their windows. This might have been true. In those days, grocery boys delivered and doctors made house calls, so they might have been self-imprisoned. They seemed quite different from my plump, merry, white-haired grandmother, who lived with my grandfather. These women were alone.

My friends and I believed they were witches. On a dare, I once made myself sneak up to the porch of one of these homes. I was terrified, but pretended to be brave. I believed that witches stole children, as in *Hansel and Gretel,* but told myself that with my friends waiting on the sidewalk, I was safe as long as I didn't let the witch entice me inside. I peeked in the window next to the door and suddenly there she was, only an inch or two on the other side of the glass, staring back at me.

I ran as fast as I could, not just to the sidewalk but all the way home. It wasn't fear that made me run, it was shame. When I saw her staring eyes, her hand against her mouth, her total fragility, I knew she was more afraid of me than I could ever be of her. I felt as guilty as I did the morning I drove my bicycle into our garage and unwittingly frightened a robin, who flew to his death against the far wall. I didn't mean to scare either the robin or the old lady.

I told the other kids, when they caught up with me, "There wasn't anybody there." I thought about her for a long time, and changed my daily route to school to avoid passing her home. It wasn't just her age that made her vulnerable, even to children. It was that she lived alone. And now I am her, a white-haired old lady, alone.

I never lived alone before. In fact, in my sixty-seven years of life before my husband's death, I always lived in homes that teemed with people. During my childhood, seven of us shared our home. There was never loneliness, nor was there simple privacy. No one knocked on a bedroom or bathroom door before entering.

When I became a mother, I maintained the old pattern, because I'd never known anything else. Ours was the house where the neighborhood children gathered, and they wandered happily into all our rooms. We had cement floors without rugs, so the children could roller-skate through the house in winter. I remember once, when I was taking a shower, my son and four of his friends all squeezed into the bathroom to ask me if it was a ball or a strike when the batter bent over purposely to make himself smaller. It didn't occur to my son that I had a right to be alone in the bathroom, nor did it occur to me to lock the door.

After my children were grown, I lived with my second husband, Bob Goulding, at our Western Institute for Group and Family Therapy, which we shared with groups of therapists-in-training. They ate with us, drank early morning coffee at our table, and never stopped talking to us from morning until late at night. Of course, they didn't come into our bedroom. By then I did believe in locks. Bob was as unaccustomed to privacy as I was, and he wanted me with him all the time. If he didn't immediately find me, he'd bellow "Mary!" at the top of his lungs, until I came running. I liked this. It felt normal and was evidence that he cared. For sixty-seven years I was scarcely ever alone in my home. Then Bob died. I moved into a two-room apartment in San Francisco, and I let my hair stay white.

When I caught glimpses of my reflection in a store window, I saw an old lady, the kind I used to call a witch, whose thin white hair trembled in the breeze. Although I insisted on wearing jeans and T-shirts like my granddaughters, instead of the long, dark dresses worn by the old widows of my youth, my age couldn't be hidden. I didn't stay indoors in the daytime and had no potted geraniums to sit behind, but at night I was usually alone in my apartment.

I began writing because I had to. I didn't know any other way to straighten out my crazy, lonely experiences. As a therapist I'd helped many people cope with the disaster of the death of a life partner, and now I was up against it.

I needed answers to some questions: How could I cope with grief? Loneliness? Retirement unshared with the husband who'd worked so long beside me? Would I end up just sitting, waiting for time to pass? Would I amble on? Run or walk? Suicide? If I chose to stay alive, how could I complete a life story that would be interesting to me? To anyone?

I read every book I could find on being widowed. Ever since I learned to read, I have looked to books to help me build my life. Books were my treasures almost from the start. And now, they didn't give me much. The books on how to be a widow or how to come to terms with grief didn't express the alienated agony I felt even in the company of friends. I couldn't endure rules or suggestions on how to cope, and threw the books aside. I turned to poetry, where I found solace and understanding and permission to grieve. Poetry spoke to my soul. I placed a favorite quotation before each chapter.

I want to share what I have learned with readers everywhere, including curious children who may still wonder if we old ladies are witches. Perhaps they will learn that we old ones feel and yearn and continue to live as fully as we know how.

For those who have not experienced the death of a partner, my wish is that they treasure fully the loves they still have. For widows and widowers, who are working out for themselves how to mourn and at the same time go on with living, I hope this book encourages them to be patient and loving to themselves. I hope they will find that even after tragedy, life can be an adventure.

Of all gods Death alone
Disdaineth sacrifice:
No man hath found or shown
The gift that Death would prize.
In vain are songs or sighs,
Paean, or praise, or moan;
Alone beneath the skies
Hath Death no altar stone!
—Aeschylus, "Death"

Death

For a long time now, Bob and I haven't been able to lie in bed facing each other, kissing and looking and touching front to front. The last time was months ago, when I persuaded him to let me wheel him back to our bedroom and our king-size bed. He said the trip was too hard. He didn't enjoy it, and I spoiled it for myself by realizing that this was probably the last time we'd be together in our own bed.

Now he lies in the hospital bed in the study. At night I sleep twelve feet away on a single bed in the living room. The study is his favorite room. The hand-carved fireplace was supposedly brought to this house from a castle in Scotland. Under the mantel it says, East, West, Home's Best, and he's always believed this to be true. His books line the wall where he used to sit with his elbows propped on his table. He sat leaning forward to help himself breathe, and from that position he could see anyone who came in through the front door or the patio entrance. He could also see the garden, the ocean fifteen miles away, and the oil painting of me as a young girl, which he particularly liked. He'd had it moved from the living room to the study and asked me to buy a light to illuminate it. He said he looked at it when I wasn't around. Now he can't see much of anything because his cataracts have gotten so much worse, and he's not a candidate for surgery.

Tonight he is feeling especially lousy. "I've never felt sicker in my life," he says, and asks that his oxygen be turned up higher. It is already as high as it will go.

"Do you have pain? Where's your pain?" I scream to make him hear.

"Everywhere. Nowhere. It's not pain. I just feel so sick." During the past two years he's had a great deal of pain from broken ribs, strained muscles in his chest, diverticulitis, and who knows what.

"Then it's probably the flu." I, the non-doctor in the family, need a banal diagnosis to give myself some measure of security. When an illness has a banal name, it is somehow tamed. There's less chance it will leap up and get you. Flu was my diagnosis for the stomach distress I'd felt the past two nights, and Doc, the man who helps take care of Bob in the daytime, is home today with a self-diagnosed flu. "If you've got the same thing I've had, it's only bad one day. You'll feel better by morning," I scream. I've never heard of anyone dying of the flu since 1918, so there is nothing really to worry about, except, of course, there is always something that terrifies me about his illnesses.

It seems that every day there are new symptoms and new worsening of old symptoms. I worry that his incapacitation will increase beyond what can be handled here at home because, no matter what, I have promised him that he will never go to a nursing home and never again to a hospital. He spent nine days last summer in intensive care with intestinal bleeding, which finally stopped. He says those were the worst days in his entire life. He won't go back for any reason.

For most of the past two years, I've worried that he would die and, recently, that he wouldn't. I am exhausted and want him to die for his sake and also to set me free. And I want him to live and live, to be with me for the rest of my life.

He says he feels too sick for dinner. "Just give me a couple of cookies." He hates to be fed but can no longer manage a fork or spoon, because his hands shake and his fingers don't work well. He can't sit up even for meals, and eating while curled on his side is hard. As he clutches the cookie between finger and thumb, his thin, blotched hand is like the pincers of a crab.

He decides he doesn't want the cookies either. It's about 6:00 P.M. "Just give me a Manhattan."

I fix his Manhattan, which he takes with a hospital straw. To assuage any internal conflict over bringing him alcohol at this stage in his illness, I paraphrase Dylan Thomas. "You don't have to go sober into that good night. You can drink against the dying of the light." He has so little left in life.

Because of the cataracts, he has stopped reading. He gets no joy from television. The last program he watched was the Super Bowl. He bitches, "What the hell am I supposed to do until baseball starts?" For him there is nothing left on television worth the struggle of almost seeing. As if that weren't enough, in the past three weeks his hearing suddenly went too. His physician came to the house to look in his ears and found wax buildup and a mild infection. Cleaning out the wax and treating the infection didn't help. I frantically tried to get an ear doctor for him, but none would make house calls, and he says he is much too weak to take an ambulance to a doctor's office. "I made house calls in the middle of raging blizzards (in North Dakota forty years ago when he was a physician doing general practice)," he reminds me angrily. "What's the matter with these doctors, anyway?"

His body has become his torturer, while his mind is clear. Many people minimize his problems because he can still bellow at them with enthusiasm or fury, depending on the subject at hand. He still offers excellent psychiatric consultation to therapists who come to him with questions about a client.

This is my beloved on February 12, 1992.

He takes a couple of sips of his manhattan and falls asleep. I go to the living room to read. About 8:00 P.M. he awakens. "Mary, Mary! I think I'm going to vomit!" I get him a wastebasket and then sit beside his bed and stroke his face. He asks if I want to get in bed with him, and I certainly do. Day and night he lies curled on his right side, so I squeeze into bed behind him, curving my body to fit his. I kiss his lovely, smooth, young shoulders and the soft skin on the back of his neck. Most of him is weathered and saggy and old, but those spots stay young. With his free left hand he reaches back to touch my hair. He's so very feeble I scarcely experience his touch. After a while, he says, "That's enough," and I get up.

In another hour he is more obviously sick. Not nauseated, but so deeply asleep that he seems to be in and out of consciousness. He was like this several times before when he had pneumonia and again this Thanksgiving when the cause was not diagnosed. Each time he survived, so I believe he will survive tonight. However, when he wakes, I ask, "Shouldn't I call a doctor?" He says, "No. They might take me to the hospital." I hold his head and kiss his face. "How sick are you, honey?"

"I don't know. Just hold me and don't let anyone come." He shuts his eyes, avoiding more talk.

When he is asleep again or unconscious—I can't tell which—I phone my daughter, who is a nurse. She has no good ideas except to do whatever makes him comfortable, and I tell her not to come over. I go back to sit beside his bed. I'm wanting him to live and am bargaining with fate. I whisper, "I'm not ready yet. Please, just one more night." I feel crazy for wanting him to die and not wanting that at all. "Love, can you hear me?" I shout, but he's on his own schedule and doesn't respond.

About 10:00 P.M. he's awake again, asking for supper. He says he feels better and is no longer nauseated. Relieved, I go into the kitchen and make us each a sandwich. I cut his into tiny pieces that he can hold.

When I get back, it's obvious he can't eat. He's barely conscious. I kiss him, and he smiles and pats my hand. I get into his bed and reach across to hold him.

We've talked of death in generalities. He hopes there's an afterlife. I have no hope. We've talked of practicalities, like where the life insurance policies may be hidden. He suggested I tell the companies they were lost in the earthquake, since neither of us has the slightest idea where they are. We've talked a bit about his dying, although it certainly isn't his favorite subject. He said he won't commit suicide because that would go against all he has taught in Redecision therapy. For months he had the means at his bedside, but chose not to overdose. He told friends, "I'm just lying here waiting to die." He said to me, "I want to go to sleep and not wake up." And at the same time, he's fought death hard.

We've cried together many times. We also laugh. Just last night, when a friend phoned to ask, "How are you?" Bob was in the midst of a hard coughing spell. He croaked out, "Dying," and added "Now!" When he hung up, we both started laughing like naughty kids at the way he'd terrified his friend. So we laugh and cry, but never say good-bye, because we always plan to be together tomorrow.

By midnight I know he's dying. I wonder how I know. Perhaps it's a slight difference in the feel of his body. My face is against his back. The only sound around us is the hissing of the oxygen. He doesn't respond to any touch. I begin to scream, "Come back!" between love words. I become more and more hysterical, until I realize that he may be hearing me somewhere deep inside himself and may be disturbed by my distress. He doesn't need that. "It's OK to go gently," I tell him, then add, "but please live if you can."

I get out of bed very quietly and walk to the office to collect all the bills that have arrived so far this month. Up to now, I haven't had time to look at them. I bring them to his table in the study, and quiet myself by writing checks. I tell myself this is something I won't be wanting to do in the days after his death, and they do have to be paid. Very carefully I staple the bills to the check receipts, and then I get back in his bed, put an arm around him, and hold his hand. Maybe I fall asleep. The next thing I know, we are both wet from his urine.

I have a difficult time stripping the bed, because he seems so much heavier. He is breathing very shallowly through his mouth, not using the oxygen at all. He's definitely comatose and dying. I put the oxygen tube in his mouth, because I think I should. I wash his body for the same reason, take the bedclothes to the laundry room, and come back.

The entire room is dead. Nothing moves. The oxygen squirts invisibly into nothing. His skin is still pink, his face relaxed, and nothing in him moves at all. There is no stillness quite like this. I know that Bob is dead. I phone our land manager, who lives only a hundred yards away. I can't bear the truth, so I hear myself sobbing, "Bob's dying." He says, "I'll be right there."

It's a little after 3:00 A.M. I come back from the phone and try to make the bed, but I can't get a sheet under him. Finally, I realize it doesn't matter, so I simply cover him with the clean sheet. And then, before the neighbor arrives, I comb Bob's beautiful white hair.

His death does separate us. My death will not bring us together again. That is how things are.
—Simone de Beauvoir, at Jean-Paul Sartre's funeral

Funeral

The funeral was held on February 16. I have little memory of the days between Bob's death and his funeral. People came and went and I must have talked with them. It was probably at the funeral parlor that somebody collected the facts of Bob's life for the obituaries. All I remember was that I told someone about my mother, who carefully filed complete obituaries for herself and my father sometime before either died. At the time of her death, we asked Dad when she had done this, and of course he didn't know. Had she assumed that no further newsworthy events were likely to occur in their lives? Although she had died suddenly and unexpectedly, everything was in order as always. All of their clothes were washed, ironed, mended, and put away. Whatever we needed, such as stamps and envelopes and extra pens, were in exactly the same place where they had always been, and the entire house was clean and orderly.

For months I had known Bob was dying, and in no way was I prepared. Besides the usual disarray, I hadn't the foggiest notion who to call or what to do. I had to be led to a funeral parlor, led through the facts for the obituary, and led back home.

Then suddenly, I began to rush. Frenzied, distraught, perhaps even rather crazy although I talked calmly enough to everyone, I began to throw out just about anything I got my hands on. I stuffed all Bob's clothing and much of mine into huge plastic garbage bags, and had my son take them to a friend who distributed clothes to farm laborers. I later learned that one of my daughters and one of Bob's sons hid behind the garage and went through these bags, secretly taking some of Bob's best wool shirts and other treasured items for themselves.

I insisted that the rented hospital furniture be removed immediately, and screamed on the phone that I was "giving away everything that was still here by 8:00 A.M. tomorrow." I phoned Salud Para La Gente, a medical group for the poor, and told them they could have every sickroom appliance Bob had owned, the electric wheelchair, potty chair, everything, if they would come right now. Without asking if they were usable, I threw away hundreds of dollars worth of drugs, because of a childhood belief that sick people's medicines spread disease. What did I think the recipient would catch? Emphysema? Old age?

Three days before the funeral, I moved all the chairs into the living room for the service, even though they had to be moved back into the dining areas immediately, so family and friends could sit down to eat. I moved them back and forth several times. I went through Bob's computer, erasing whatever hadn't already been erased, because the computer was going to one of his sons. I piled up copies of some of the papers he had written, to give away at the funeral, and threw out reams of other people's work.

I couldn't stop. At night, when everyone else slept, I continued the dismantling. Later I wondered why I had no copies of the obituaries from local newspapers, and then realized that I must have thrown them out, too.

While Bob was ill, we weeded through our psychology library, giving away the texts we didn't want. Now I sent cartons of books to the used bookstores, insisting that they be taken out of the house immediately. I gave away all of Bob's mysteries and science fiction, and then I decided I no longer wanted our Transactional Analysis library, which included every T.A. book that had ever been published, most of them personally inscribed to us by the authors. They went to India and are now in a "Goulding Library" in New Delhi.

As I dumped our possessions, my mood alternated between grief and angry desperation. I hated every leftover evidence of our life and work together. I didn't have Bob, so what good were our belongings? Without Bob, I didn't want accumulated evidence even of my own professional life.

Bob's family began to arrive the day before the funeral. Although they were tender and loving, I was mostly unaware of them, except when their voices became intrusive. I felt trapped by their chatter and by my own need to respond politely with irrelevant words. At the same time that I shared my plans to move to San Francisco and travel to Costa Rica, I wondered how I could survive even the next half hour. My sweetest love was forever dead.

My sister Laurie Barrett came from Wisconsin. I didn't know how important her presence would be until I saw her walk through the door. I told her by telephone that the distance was too great, and she shouldn't take the time from her work. Then there she was, my friend and my security in this bleak time.

The day of the funeral, I moved the chairs again. Many family members offered to help, then backed away as they realized I wanted to do this job alone. I placed the wooden box with Bob's ashes on the mantel, hung his portrait above it, and put flower arrangements on mantels and tables. The place felt deathly bare. I needed lots and lots more flowers, every room crammed with them. I ordered more and phoned a friend to beg her to bring some. She came with armloads of cut roses, Bob's favorite flowers, and stuck them everywhere.

I now know that I will always send flowers to funerals. Why should giving to a favorite charity mean making a funeral even more bleak than it naturally is?

For me, the funeral was appalling. In spite of my carting around the furniture, I didn't let myself notice that there weren't nearly enough chairs. No one had suggested renting more, so most of the people had to stand through what began as a lovely testament by friends and family and then continued interminably. Finally, I told the primary speaker to stop talking. I had no idea what had been said.

Even worse than the ceremony was the burial of the ashes. I wasn't aware of what I wanted until it was too late to change the plans. As everyone went outside to witness the burial of his ashes beside a new redwood tree that Bob asked to have planted in his memory, I yearned to grab the box and run away. I wanted to keep the ashes with me a little longer, to be alone with them for at least another day.

Bob and I were alone together when he died. Too late, I knew that this is how the final act, the burial, should have been. Just me and what was left of him. I wanted to dig my own hole and bury the ashes whenever it felt right to me, after everyone had gone. I wanted to see and touch those ashes instead of just putting the box into the ground. But the box was already being carried out, and I told myself that this was a normal way to end a funeral service. His brother, his grown children, his grandchildren, his friends and colleagues were also mourners, who had the right to participate in his burial.

I suffered as the box of ashes was set in the hole and covered with dirt. Afterward his family sang out his goofy high school cheer, which was a family tradition whenever they were all together.

Everyone went back inside, and undoubtedly I spoke and hugged appropriately. I looked at the buffet table, and I think I complimented the people who put it together. I ate the food. By then I had disappeared inside myself. I was numb, not there. Later, reading over the list of mourners, I discovered best friends who had come long distances. Though I must have greeted them, I have no memory of their presence.

My sister Laurie left, and by the next morning everyone had gone. As the last car drove away, I stood alone in the driveway, a stiff old lady, silently resenting everything.

I considered digging up the ashes, but what use, really, would that have been? What use are ashes anyway? I got ready to leave for San Francisco that afternoon. I have no memory of who drove me there.

I had already left my home when the death certificate arrived: "Robert Lawrence Goulding, Caucasian, son of Albert Goulding and Miriam Fleck, died on February 13, 1992, at 03:15 of cardiac arrest due to respiratory arrest due to emphysema."

It's little I care what path I take
And where it leads it's little I care;
But out of this house, lest my heart break,
I must go, and off somewhere.
—Edna St. Vincent Millay, "Departure"

Leaving

I spared myself the misery that many widows and widowers endure, of remaining in their homes after the funeral guests have departed. It must be intolerable to sit in one's usual chair with no one in the other chair; to sleep alone in a bed meant for two; to fix a meal and bring it to the table where no one is waiting to eat with you; to wander about a house that feels eternally empty.

I was always phobic about being alone in the country after dark, especially in an isolated institute like ours. It was large, on the side of a mountain, with twenty acres between it and the nearest neighbor. When Bob had traveled without me, which was rare, I either stayed with family or took a vacation. During our last months together, when Bob couldn't even get out of bed without my help, I became frightened as soon as the sun went down. I slept with the burglar alarm under my pillow and kept waking up with each new noise. I was well-known for curing phobias in others, but had not cured my own. I hated being alone in the country and was always content and safe in a city.

My grandfather grew up on Clark Street beside the streetcar tracks in the neighborhood made famous by Nelson Algren's *Man with the Golden Arm.* He and my grandmother lived there until my officious aunt persuaded them to come to the suburbs, where it was pleasant and quiet, and the grandchildren were nearby. That move lasted three months, and then my grandfather proclaimed, "We're going back to Chicago. A person can't sleep here, with all the noise from the damned crickets," and returned to his home beside the streetcar lines. Someday I suppose the researchers will isolate the gene responsible for his choice. It must exist in me, as well.

The institute was a perfect place for us during our years of teaching together, but that life was over, and I would not stay there after the funeral. Friends loaned me their condo in San Francisco. My sister Bette Kreger was in Taiwan when Bob died, and had just returned. She and her husband, Bill, flew to San Francisco to help me find a permanent apartment for myself. Again I felt the strength of family. I was still numb, so we had a good time together in the city, as we searched for a place for me to live.

I found a two-room apartment on the twentieth floor of a huge apartment complex overlooking the San Francisco Bay, complete with swimming pool and spa. There was a supermarket just below my apartment, and a bank, post office, international movie house, and public transportation within a block or two. During the twenty-two years Bob and I lived at the institute, I had to drive fifteen miles just to buy a newspaper. This was exactly what I wanted.

The apartment in San Francisco was available on April first. I had to find a place to live until then, and didn't want to intrude on friends or family. I needed to be alone. Although I planned to wait several months before traveling, I bought a round-trip ticket to Costa Rica by way of Miami, hired a realtor to sell our institute, and left. I would study Spanish to keep my mind off my grief. I chose to be as far away as possible from anything that reminded me of my life with Bob. I knew no one in Costa Rica, and that was what I wanted. I was still numb. I didn't feel much of anything until my bag was stolen in Miami.

While waiting for the limousine to take me to the airport at Miami, en route to Costa Rica, I left my two carry-on bags with the bellhop at the Miami Holiday Inn, and went to buy a *New York Times.* When I returned a couple of minutes later, one bag had been stolen. It contained all my diabetic paraphernalia—insulin and needles and blood glucose meter—plus my fins, mask, and snorkel. My plane to Costa Rica was leaving in a little over two hours, and I was due at the airport in twenty minutes.

I, who never cried in public, began to wail. While a desk clerk at the Holiday Inn was phoning the police, I heard myself say, "A policeman won't do me any good." What I meant was, no one could help me. I felt lost, unprotected, and appallingly alone. I was abandoned. The impact of Bob's death finally caught up with me.

During the months I watched over Bob as he grew more and more frail, I grew accustomed to the knowledge that I would be alone. I knew many people loved me. My children loved me. Many friends, including innumerable therapists, cared about me. But no one loved me the way Bob did. No one would ever again love me as he did.

Hotel personnel fluttered about me. A policeman arrived. I wanted to go home, but I had no home. I didn't want to go to Costa Rica, but I had nowhere else in the world to go. I continued wailing.

Then a part of me came to my rescue. I heard myself insisting that they call the airport to tell them I'd be checking in late; find me a doctor; drive me to the doctor's office for the prescriptions I needed; get me to a pharmacy, where I could replace my diabetic equipment and medicine; drive me to a sport store to replace my mask, snorkel, and fins; and make certain I was at the airport on time to catch my plane. The personnel at the Holiday Inn did exactly as I asked. They must have been quite frightened as they tried to deal with a seemingly incompetent old lady who gave orders while sobbing helplessly.

At the doctor's office, his secretary said I would have to wait, and my wailing increased until she brought him to me. At that point I told him exactly what prescriptions to write. I did explain, "My husband died and I'm not myself," and kept right on crying. He wrote rapidly, handed me the prescriptions, rushed me into the hotel car, and refused payment. I wailed more loudly than ever on the way to the pharmacy, but made sure I got what I needed, although seemingly undergoing a severe personality disintegration. I was functioning and not functioning simultaneously. Later it amazed me that I actually went in that condition to a sports shop and replaced my snorkeling gear. I was still wailing as I got on the plane.

In the past I always traveled eagerly. Now I shut my eyes so I wouldn't have to communicate with anyone. I hurt physically throughout my body. It was as if I had been beaten up. I also hurt in my soul, whatever and wherever it was.

It is possible to talk about him with someone, but to think of him when one is alone, to evoke his image, is unbearably painful.
—Anton Chekhov, "Heartache"

Costa Rica

When I arrived at the San Jose, Costa Rica, airport, I asked a cab driver to take me to a decent, interesting, cheap hotel. I always found this more effective than making reservations. Hotels chosen through travel literature were often disappointing. Once publicized, the "lovely little treasures" became overpriced tourist traps.

The driver chose La Gema, a pleasant place with an interior patio filled with tables. The European guests sat around, eating, drinking beer, and exchanging information about Costa Rica. Everyone told me the best beach was at Manuel Antonio National Park.

I took off by bus to the Pacific coast the next morning. The beach was fine, with warm water, good waves, smooth sand, and many monkeys in the jungle just behind it. The birds were singing everywhere in the jungle and on the beach, but that only made me more grief stricken. I'd always been an exuberant traveler, and now I couldn't recognize myself. I went swimming, walked through the jungle, and even rented a small board for riding the waves. Then I gave up the pretense of being a happy tourist and took the bus back.

I holed up in La Gema for a couple of days, sobbing in my room and taking solitary walks about the city. I bought a pair of cheap, reflecting dark glasses so no one would see my tears.

San Jose was hot and uninteresting. The buildings were old, mostly one or two stories, faded, with nothing particularly appealing in the windows. It was a Latin city with no Indian culture. A small tourist market in the center of town had the same handicrafts that can be found in San Francisco, imported from Guatemala, Peru, and Ecuador.

There were positives. No one shouted or shoved or whispered obscenities, as in some foreign capitals. Even the pretty, young female tourists weren't whistled at or pinched. It was a decent place with far fewer beggars than in San Francisco, and none of the obviously psychotic homeless wandering untreated in the streets that San Francisco had in such appalling numbers. People looked at each other and smiled. This was a land of peace, with no army since 1948. The literacy rate was one of the highest in the world, far higher than ours. Ecology was everyone's passion. In my bleak mood, I considered Costa Rica to be healthy, admirable, and dull.

I found the two language schools near the national university that were advertised in the United States newspapers, asked to visit their advanced classes, and was not impressed. Upon further investigation, I discovered a language institute a few blocks from the hotel in San Jose, and a Spanish professor who became my teacher, friend, confidant, and therapist without portfolio.

Carlos was a handsome, stocky man about forty-five years old, with brown eyes, dark hair, and a mustache. His speech was musical and very clear. He smiled a lot and loved to invent jokes. After watching him work, I signed up to join two other students in his advanced class in the mornings, and to take private lessons from him in the afternoons.

His classroom, like much of Costa Rica, was shabby by our standards. He had a tiny room with a large blackboard on one wall, a table with six chairs crowded around it, and a noisy but essential fan near the window. He'd enlivened the walls with slogans, advice, and jokes in Spanish, plus an incredible, hand-lettered index of over a hundred items of Spanish grammar.

That first morning we three students chatted with Carlos in broken Spanish about—among other subjects—our jobs, our hobbies, and what we thought of the upcoming elections in the United States. All four of us spoke entirely in Spanish. Carlos introduced new topics every few minutes and, teaching cheerfully from our mistakes, continuously praised us.

Then came the afternoon and the private sessions. "Tell me something of your life," Carlos said. I began to sob and apologize at the same time. "I am sorry. My husband died. I am sorry. I don't want to cry."

"It is natural to cry because of this."

"I don't want to."

He ran both his hands through his thick, curly hair in a nervous gesture that I got to know well, and leaned intently across the table toward me. His expression was very concerned. "I think it is healthy to cry when you are sad. You are a psychotherapist. Isn't it healthy?"

"Of course." I smiled. More relaxed, I talked about Bob's illness and death. There were many words I didn't know, such as "lungs" and "emphysema." When I was stuck, I wrote words in English, which occasionally he understood, and I gestured. He filled in the Spanish words I lacked.

In spite of what he'd said, I continued apologizing for my tears. "I hate to cry in front of strangers. I feel embarrassed."

He said, "In my church, when I understood for the first time in my life that God is a Father who loves me, I cried for hours. I cried and cried. I could not stop crying. I was embarrassed, too."

"Thank you for telling me," I told him. "You are a good man." Then, because it was suddenly very important to me to keep our exchanges genuine, I told him my position. I didn't know the word for atheist. I said, "You believe in God. I am happy for you. I do not believe. I do not believe in life after death. I do not believe that I will be with Bob again—ever—anywhere."

"How hard for you," he said with his extraordinary sweetness.

That was our beginning. As we continued talking to each other, I realized how much I needed someone other than family or friends to listen to me.

Every morning our small group laughed and learned. Carlos showed us cartoons from local papers to see if we understood them. He offered games he had invented and dozens of assorted packages of his handwritten flash cards, so we could use new words and new phrases. He wrote the rules of grammar one by one on the blackboard, giving examples and then quizzing us. After each mini-lesson, he'd erase the board in grand swirls of chalk dust. I was able to compartmentalize my grief, so that the other students, though they knew I was a widow, did not hear my sorrow. They were young businessmen, and I didn't want to open up to them.

Each afternoon I talked about Bob. I gave a myriad of details: his food preferences, his politics, and the way he argued loudly with the coaches' decisions during televised football and baseball games.

I practiced new adjectives by describing Bob. He was talented, astute, wise, and intelligent. "I think he was the best psychiatrist in the United States." He was very kind. When he was angry, he shouted. When he was sad, he cried. He was not embarrassed to cry. He was happy—no, that is not the right word—he loved life. He was a lover of life. Do you say that in Spanish? He loved me always.

In that sweltering room in Costa Rica, I talked and talked about Bob. I told Carlos how much we loved each other; how we worked, played, argued, and were always together. I told him about the long, hard months of Bob's illness. "Even when he was very sick, when he was in bed all day, he gave money to friends to buy me presents. He told them what to buy for me." Carlos would interrupt to correct my grammar and offer new words.

He also responded to what I was saying. He said, "I envy you.

You had a beautiful love." Another time he said, "You two were so intimate with each other. My wife and I are not that intimate."

Later he reported, "I told my wife about you and Bob. I told her that I want our marriage to be more like yours. She says I never listen to her, so I said I would try to do it. She doesn't listen to me either, but I was a hero and didn't tell her that." We both laughed.

I asked him to tell me more about himself, and he did, proudly. He grew up in an impoverished family, with an alcoholic, abusive father, an ineffectual mother, and uncles who were very cruel to him. In spite of this treatment, he worked hard and was the first person in his entire family to graduate from high school and go to college.

He had a wife, who didn't work outside the home, and four children. He was a loving father and never abusive. As a young adult, he drank excessively but now used no alcohol. "I will never let my children see me drunk." He smiled as he bragged about the intelligence of his children and the As they received in school.

He was very earnest, an ardent member of a fundamentalist sect, and politically conservative. I found it strange that we, so different, deeply appreciated each other. He found it strange, too. I taught him the English term "soul mates."

Sometimes we used the language studies to flirt with each other. He said, "If I had known you when I was young, I would have asked you to marry me." I responded with a more simple form, "And if I were a young woman, I would want a romance with you right now." We both giggled.

To keep our relationship proper, he continued to call me Doña Mary.

I was accustomed to the verbal informality of Mexican friends, and found "doña" to be quaint. But I accepted the word and sometimes called him "señor" in return. Perhaps I was now so old that even in Mexico I would be a "doña," a respected ancient one.

My lighthearted flirting caused an unwelcome internal phenomenon, strong sexual feelings toward him. I was appalled. How could I be sexual with Bob dead? I knew that this was common in bereavement. I told others that sexual appetite immediately after the death of a lover is an affirmation of a life force: "I am alive, whether or not I truly desire to live."

Almost two years ago I turned off sexually. Unable to breathe naturally and with his body skin so tender that even light touches hurt his penis, Bob still offered to pleasure me. It was heartbreaking. I didn't consciously stop wanting him sexually. I insisted, and believed, that my lack of sexual desire was a reaction to my own diabetes and had nothing to do with his illness. Now I was proved wrong.

I didn't tell Carlos any of this. I believed that he would have been shocked at the thought that an old lady could feel sexual desire and doubly shocked that a woman older than his mother would even fantasize having sex with him. Whether or not he would have been shocked, it was certainly true that I was projecting onto him my own horror at myself. I remembered working with several widows and with surviving partners of AIDS victims, all of whom had trouble believing that their new surges of sexuality, immediately following the death of their partner, were decent and healthy. I was now in the same state.

I left for a three-day visit to the Tortuguero area, and this time my trip was better than my gloomy visit to the Pacific coast. I enjoyed riding in a small, quiet boat on calm jungle rivers with a guide who pointed out parrots, monkeys, and even a crocodile. The next morning I got up early and walked alone into the jungle. Suddenly, I heard growling animals all around me. It was as if dozens of lions were encircling the path. I knew from the day before that I was hearing howler monkeys; scrawny little things with incredible voice power. As I got closer I could watch their antics. They leaped, seeming to fly from branch to branch, ate fruit high above me, and threw the large seeds all over the floor of the jungle. They howled with what seemed pure exuberance in being alive.

Watching them, my own excitement changed to guilt. As a therapist who had dealt with survivors, I knew what was going on with me. I felt guilty for having sexual impulses, and now I felt guilty for enjoying this trip. Even though my guilt was absurd, I didn't feel right about delighting in this wonderful jungle without Bob.

On the way back to the lodge, I was lucky enough to encounter a group of tiny red frogs hopping near my path. I was careful not to become too excited or enthusiastic, even though I knew that this was a rare treat that very few people see, even here.

My studies at the institute continued. With six hours of Spanish a day, I was learning rapidly and could now communicate quite well. I told Carlos everything that I later put into my biography of Bob, *Sweet Love Remembered.*

Carlos talked about some of the tragedies of his childhood, and I helped him drop the guilt he carried because he couldn't cure his family or protect himself or other family victims, when he was just a boy. I counseled him on being a psychotherapist with members of his church, who were already coming to him for advice. He was obviously a natural therapist. Without him, I don't know how I could have dealt with this first stage of being a widow. He gave me the freedom to say whatever I chose, to feel my grief, and to sob instead of choking back tears. He was always there for me and, best of all, he was emotionally genuine. I was impressed and grateful that he never tried to convert me to his belief in God. He accepted my atheism as I accepted his fundamentalism.

At our second-to-last session together, he asked, "What do you do when a person is afraid of heights?"

"Who? You?"

"Yes." He explained he was comfortable in this office on the second floor, but was very uncomfortable on the fourth floor, where the staff held their meetings. He was afraid to sit by the window or to look out.

"OK, come on. You and I are going to cure you." I asked him to stand in front of the window on the second floor. I stood beside him. Below us, the street was crowded with cars and pedestrians. "Are you OK here?"

"Yes."

"Good." I pointed outside. "Look down. Are you still OK?"

When he said he was fine, I asked him to imagine that his mother and father were standing on the sidewalk below. "Tell them, 'I am not going to jump,' and discover if that is true."

"Oh, yes, that is true. I would never try to kill myself or hurt myself. 'I am not going to jump.'"

"Perfect. Now tell them, 'I'm not going to fall.'"

This time he stiffened, looking very tense. "I just remembered something. I think it is the problem." He explained that his mother was always terrified that he would fall. For example, when he wanted to climb trees, she'd scream at him to get down before he fell and injured himself. "She tried to protect me."

I said, "How sad. You are a little boy, and she does not protect you from your father. She does not protect you from important things. You need protection from the dangerous people in your life, from real dangers. And she only protects you from imaginary dangers, like trees or this window."

He had tears in his eyes. "I was never protected. No one protected me, and I needed protection." He thought about it. "Could I have taken care of myself in trees? I suppose I could have. I have taken care of myself for years!" He was very excited. Laughing, he yelled to me, "Come on, we're going to the fourth floor!" Usually, he walked quite sedately to the elevator. This time we ran up the stairs.

On the fourth floor, we went to the faculty room, and he stood at the window, looking down. "I am not afraid!"

I told him that his was the fastest cure in history, and he was delighted. He said he was going home, as soon as my lesson was finished, to tell his wife.

During our last session, we talked about what he had done, and went back to the fourth floor. He was not afraid. I explained, "Bob taught me how to cure height phobias. This was a gift from him to you."

We said we would miss each other. I asked, "Will you permit me to give you an embrace?" He hurried around the table, and we hugged good-bye.

Come to me in the silence of the night;
Come in the speaking silence of a dream...
Come back to me in dreams, that I may give
Pulse for pulse, breath for breath;
Speak low, lean low,
As long ago, my love, how long ago.
—Christina Rossetti, "Echo"

San Francisco

My family met me at the airport and drove me back to what had been Bob's and my home, our Western Institute in Watsonville, California. Our land manager, Dennis King; two of Bob's daughters, Kathleen Callahan and Kelley Riley; my son, David Edwards; my two daughters, Karen Edwards and Claudia Pagano; and the grandchildren were all on hand to help me pack and move to San Francisco.

The hot tub was turned on, the grandchildren got out the golf cart and drove it all over the property, and Karen identified the exotic weed that only grows in our area and was recently labeled endangered. Jokes alternated with political arguments. It was almost like old times and would have been great fun if Bob were there too. I avoided the new redwood tree where his ashes were, because I didn't want to cry in the presence of family, even though I knew they'd understand.

We walked through the eighteen rooms, deciding what I would take with me to my new two rooms: the bedroom set that belonged to my parents, because Bob's and mine was too large for my city bedroom; the horrendously ugly but comfortable electric lounge chair that my father used before he died; a couch and chair from a condo I'd owned by the ocean; six tiny, uncomfortable antique dining room chairs and our dining table. "When the institute is sold," I told them all, "I'll buy furniture I like."

I chose to keep my favorite paintings, plus my enlarged photographs from Bali and Switzerland. They reminded me of vacations Bob and I had taken together. Of course, our dining room cabinet would stay with me. Bob and I bought it one beautiful, shining day, early in our marriage. Without planning to buy anything, we strolled into a warehouse with booths owned by various antique dealers.

Bob was the one who spotted the cabinet, a marvelously impressive, hand-carved antique. He asked the price, and when the dealer told him, Bob boomed out, "Why so cheap?" She explained that no one knew its history and, therefore, it wasn't possible to get a higher price for it. Bob said, "I can invent the history," and wrote out a check. "It's too big to have come by covered wagon, so let's say it came around the Horn. What's a good year?" He laughed and hugged me, shook hands with the nearby sales people, and complimented the dealer on her merchandise, her style, her hairdo, and who knows what else. The entire mall seemed invigorated by Bob's presence. That's how he was. Even though the cabinet was big and my new living room was small, I chose to keep it.

I grieved over some of the things I left behind: the two beautiful Spanish rugs in my office; all our carvings from a trip to New Guinea; the Mexican rugs; the pottery funeral scene that I bought in Oaxaca long ago, before I had any familiarity with death. After making my selections, I walked through the rooms, urging the others to take what they wanted.

That evening, I hiked around the grounds alone, while the family was in the hot tub. The redwood tree was thriving. There was no indentation in the ground to show where the box of ashes was buried, though I knew exactly where it was. Someday, after the property sold, I planned to ask the new owner if I might put a marker on the spot.

The next morning, as we were packing the rented van, my son and I had a horrendous verbal battle over nothing. I fired him, he fired me, he kept right on supervising the job, and then the quarrel was over. I was increasingly edgy and needed to get away from the institute as fast as possible.

In San Francisco we arranged the furniture, set up my computer, hung my paintings and photographs, and put away dishes, books, clothing, and the miscellaneous things I'd stuffed in boxes. Then we went swimming at the health club in the apartment complex. The next day I bought lots of bright plants for the balcony and the living room. I bought new, small picture frames and loaded my dressers with family photos, including my favorite photos of Bob and me together.

I had no regrets about leaving Watsonville. I had always loved San Francisco and knew it was where I wanted to live. I'd picked exactly the right furniture, the right art, and I was proud of what I'd accomplished. My apartment was beautiful.

Sitting on the balcony, twenty floors up, I watched the boats on the bay and knew how lucky I was to be able to afford to live here. Although I understood my sadness, I believed that I ought to be happy. This began the long season of "oughts." I ought to be cheerful. I ought to be busy. I ought to exercise and to write. I ought to begin to get over my mourning, though I had really barely begun it.

I ought to respond to all the condolence letters I'd received. Before leaving for Costa Rica, I paid our ex-secretary to answer the ones I'd already read. When I returned from Costa Rica, there were many more letters, and I began hearing that people were upset with the letters our secretary had sent. They, too, thought I ought to be writing them myself.

I cherished the letters, especially those with specific memories of Bob, but I didn't know how to respond. Nothing I could say seemed adequate. My love was dead and everyone knew it.

What more was there? I ended up sending a printed postcard with my new address, and felt ashamed.

After more than twenty-two years, I had no housekeeper and no need for one. When Bob was alive, he used to complain from time to time about dust on the bookcases or dirt collected on the top of the refrigerator, but in all those years at Western Institute, I never noticed such things. My mother was never able to find a cleaning person who cleaned well enough to satisfy her, while I never found one who didn't satisfy me. Everyone could clean a house better and faster than I could.

In my new apartment, for the first time in my life I became a fanatical housekeeper. I knew this was crazy behavior on my part, but I couldn't quit. Everything had to be perfect at all times. I kept my bathroom immaculate and didn't even use the tub, because I showered at the health club. I kept the kitchen clean by doing almost no cooking. I bought ready-to-eat food at the supermarket. The few times I did cook, I washed all the cooking utensils and put them back in place before I sat down to eat, which meant that the food was no longer hot when I got around to it. I didn't care.

I kept my clothes hung up, papers out of sight, and I immediately wiped up any spot that showed itself on a table or floor. I didn't know why I was doing this. My behavior was neurotic, and I took no particular pleasure from it. Perhaps I was keeping the apartment clean because it is so easy to do when a person lives alone. Or perhaps I wanted to keep it an anonymous, unused, perfectly polished hotel suite. I didn't really consider it my home. It seemed as if I was on a prolonged vacation, and any day I would be going back to Watsonville and Bob. When I thought rationally, I knew I had no home in Watsonville, but I had no home in San Francisco either.

With nothing in the world that I had to do, I adhered to an obsessive schedule. Every morning I read in Spanish for half an hour, then got out of bed, had breakfast, and swam a half mile in the health club pool. After the swim, I chose whether to use the sauna or the hot tub or both. I walked three miles almost every day, exploring the city. I had to put some form into a formless, purposeless life.

I became a vegetarian. Perhaps I didn't want to have any responsibility for unnecessary deaths, even of animals. Fortunately, there were no insects in the apartment, because I'd developed an intense aversion to killing anything. I carefully stepped over bugs on the streets and often watched them with a fascination I hadn't felt since childhood. Life, even theirs, was valuable.

Because dinner alone without Bob was unendurable, I stopped having dinner except with friends. Alone, I dined on popcorn at movie theaters. I tried to stay away from movies that reminded me of Bob, but I never knew which those would be. There were sharp, terrible surprises. In a lovely movie, *Danzón,* the dancer returns to the dance hall in Mexico City, after an unsuccessful search for her dance partner, and there he is—he has returned; the two of them dance together joyously—they smile and smile. I felt stricken for days with the pain those smiles brought me. Her dance partner, who was not even her love, came back to her, while my love could never return.

I was deeply grateful when anyone invited me for lunch or dinner. But when people said, "Let me know what I can do," or "Let's get together sometime," I felt a profound weariness, even when they were good friends I might have wanted to see. I didn't understand how to respond, and I couldn't find the energy to make suggestions. I didn't even want to choose a restaurant.

I wanted others to phone, offer a free meal, send over flowers and books, or write a note. One therapist sent me a loving card almost every week, with a joke or just a message about how he was getting along building his boat. I loved the mail from him. Another therapist phoned often to say, "Today I'm hiking up the hill behind my house," or "Let's walk in Golden Gate Park." Her specific suggestions brought me hours of pleasure in the midst of this very painful time.

Ruth McClendon and Les Kadis, friends and former associates at Western Institute, suggested a Monday night supper club for the three of us and anyone else we cared to invite.

Monday evenings with them were a fine distraction and later, when I became acutely depressed, their presence on Mondays was lifesaving.

It was hard to plan my life, and I felt nurtured when friends offered specific treats. I felt childlike in my need for people to take the initiative.

I wanted to be with couples, but I was often oversensitive to their love and their quarrels. Their smiles and fondness for each other reminded me that I was an outcast, banished from the world of love. If they quarreled, as Bob and I often did, I wanted desperately for them to stop. I wondered whether they had any idea that one of them would some day be alone, that the other would die. I relived the pain of Bob's months of dying each time I heard that a husband of a friend was ill or facing surgery.

Although I'd made my plans for widowhood during Bob's illness, I really didn't have a clue as to what it would be like. Neither did any of these couples I was with. They were as innocent as I was. They seemed fragile and vulnerable to me, especially if they were old and had been married many years. While laughing and talking with them, I'd find myself wondering which of them would die first. Would the survivor hurt like I did?

Even tiny, silly problems loomed large. I seemed to misplace things more frequently, and would become nearly hysterical while searching for them. Bob had always helped me search until he was bedridden. Even from his bed, he'd suggest hiding places or simply remind me, "Sweetie, it doesn't matter. Wait until it surfaces."

Sometimes I forgot invitations, even though I kept my date book beside the phone. I believed that I was forgetting people's names much more frequently, and ignored the fact that I'd had the same trouble with names when I was an undergraduate in college. I believed that I couldn't memorize Spanish words as easily as before, which was probably true. Crossword puzzles seemed more difficult. I seriously thought I was in the early stages of Alzheimer's disease. I needed Bob to refute these self-induced terrors. He used to tell me, "Go to sleep. Cancer never begins in the middle of the night, so you don't have cancer," or "You're not having a heart attack. It's only a sore muscle in your chest." After my resident physician promised I was not mortally ill, I'd sleep calmly, cuddled against him.

That was long ago, before he was so sick, before he lived in a hospital bed in the study. Now I would recall his words and the feel of him in bed with me, to calm myself when I'd begin one of my crazy concerns. It was impossible to believe that only a few years ago I'd written our book, *Not to Worry!* I was now inventing crazy worries that had no basis in reality, while refusing to consider what could be real concerns. I walked the streets of San Francisco at night, even in the notorious Tenderloin, as unconcerned about my safety as I was during my adolescence.

I overreacted to minor annoyances. I got tired of sending death certificates to banks and to credit card and insurance companies, and I began arguing over the phone with their representatives. "Do you think I'd lie about my own husband's death?" I screamed at one of them. When American Express told me I must provide a copy of the death certificate and then reapply for a credit card as a single person, I sent them my card hacked into tiny pieces. Vindictively, because of my problem with American Express, I didn't tell MasterCard that Bob had died and continued to use his gold card, issued through the American Psychiatric Association. Every month I paid "his" bills and planned spitefully to use it for the rest of my life. There was something repulsive about allowing a nameless, faceless company to have Bob's death certificate. When I ran out of certificates, I refused to get more and told people angrily, "Call Santa Cruz County and buy it for yourself."

I wrote to Bob's colleges, medical school, and professional organizations, telling them that he was dead. Most paid no attention, and continued to send mailings which I threw in the garbage unopened. His alma mater and his fraternity acknowledged his death by continuing to send their silly mailings, but now they were addressed to *Mrs.* Robert L. Goulding. I finally stopped notifying organizations of Bob's death.

The legal details of our wills were handled properly before

Bob died. Though his will did not have to go through probate, my attorney found a way to charge me a great deal more than I'd expected, so I fired him as soon as possible. From my experience, a good accountant was better than an attorney, cost less, and knew more about how to handle my shaky finances.

At first I paid no attention to money, and then was shocked to discover how rapidly I was depleting my supply. How long could I afford this apartment, if Western Institute didn't sell? I never before had to solve money problems. We could always buy whatever we wanted. I earned money, Bob earned money, we earned it together, and it all went into an anonymous pot. We had always had enough, and Bob kept our accounts.

I hated budgeting and scrimping, so I decided I would keep on living in my expensive apartment, take trips whenever I chose, and begin to work again when necessary. To hedge my bets, I found a cheap retirement home, where I could live if and when I could no longer work. My ability to teach here and abroad made me far more fortunate than most widows. Financial problems are relative. Compared to friends who had only social security, I was very fortunate.

After firing my lawyer, I cut my expenses further by firing my dentist. I decided I probably would not outlive the gold and porcelain already in my mouth. If there were cracks—as he said there were—between precious metals and root canals, I no longer believed fixing them was worth $1,000 a tooth. Since my teeth had supported innumerable dentists throughout my lifetime, giving up dentistry was a profound decision. Like most of the people in this world, from now on I would only see a dentist if something really hurt, and then I'd look for a cheap one.

When Bob died, I stopped dressing up, so I didn't need to buy clothes. However, having something new to wear cheered me when I was gloomy. I bought cheap T-shirts in bright, solid colors, and new jeans, to pretend I was not an old widow.

Nights were very sad. I was filled with longing for even a few minutes with Bob, to tell him I loved him, to hold him, to see his face and feel his body next to mine. I wanted to apologize for anything and everything. If I could do it over, I'd be a flawless wife. At night I couldn't keep from obsessing about how much I wanted him with me once more.

For the first time in my adult life, I turned on the radio at night, simply to bring another voice into the apartment. Within a few minutes, hating canned sound or becoming hysterically sad over some love song, I would turn it off again.

A friend invited me to join a small writing group at her home, and I began to write Bob's biography, *Sweet Love Remembered.* Writing about Bob gave my life a purpose. I put everything I told Carlos in Costa Rica into the book, and made it the story of our personal and professional years together. I wished I'd started the book before Bob died, so he could have brought his remembrances into it, too.

I chose the photographs and picked a bright red cover for the book. It was my valentine to his memory. The first month after publication, I sold about a thousand copies, spending every day packing them and carting them to the post office. I liked the busy work and knowing that the International Transactional Analysis Association would eventually benefit from the sales. When people phoned and wrote to tell me how much they loved the book, their words brought me real joy. I could honestly tell myself, "Bob would have liked this book." It was my memorial to him and a way of beginning to say good-bye.

I went back to the institute with my daughters, to see what I'd left behind. I looked at the New Guinea pieces, offered one to my daughter Karen, one to Bob's grandson Daniel, and one to my grandson Brian. I opened the box that contained the Mexican pottery funeral scene I'd bought in Oaxaca in 1964. I'd kept it displayed on a shelf in the office until Bob's illness became worse, and I could no longer bear a scene of death.

When I attended the Rockefeller exhibit of Mexican folk art, I realized that my pottery funeral, though not in top condition, was as fine as anything in that collection. Impetuously, I decided to give it away.

No one in the family wanted it. I remembered visiting a therapist in Texas years ago, who had a collection of Mexican folk art. I phoned her and offered to ship her my funeral scene, if she would pay the freight charges. She was delighted.

In San Francisco, my daughter Karen and I unpacked the pottery for one last look at the mourning scene. Each brightly colored figure was about nine inches tall. The dead man lay in an open box, painted bright blue with white flowers. Two pottery angels with long white dresses, long black braids, and blue-and-white painted wings, watched over him. The lone male mourner stared in stoic isolation over the dead man in the open coffin, not daring to look down. Grief-stricken female figures tried to comfort each other. One woman, holding a candle, stared curiously at the corpse. Each clay figure was unique, and all had expressions of infinite sadness.

I kept the figures on my dining room table for almost a week and photographed each piece. The prints were excellent. I thought of finding an artist who could make a collage of the photographs, or perhaps I'd have them enlarged. And do what with them? Hang them on my walls? If I wanted to have the scene with me forever, why was I giving it away?

I was giving away too many things that I really wanted. If anything I owned was painfully tied to my life with Bob, I got rid of it as fast as possible and then regretted what I'd done. I should have reminded myself of that and kept the funeral scene. Instead, I put the photos in a tiny album and sent the pottery to Texas. Almost immediately, I was horrified. I wanted them back. This is the letter I wrote asking for their return:

> *"One of the craziest aspects of my behavior since Bob died is that I keep giving things away and then grieving their loss. I don't understand why I keep doing this, and I've decided not to give anything more away no matter what. Unfortunately, I decided that before and don't seem to stop the giveaways. I no longer own a car because I've given away our two cars and our truck, when I could have sold them and used the money. I also gave away our silverware, china,*

etc. I tell people, 'Take anything you want because I don't want anything that reminds me of Bob,' and then I'm immediately sorry. Would you be willing to give me back the funeral scene? I love it and don't want to be parted from it."

Usually, I didn't burden people with my craziness. I didn't even mention my chronic sadness. Instead, I habitually told them, "I'm fine, thank you." "I'm as well as can be expected, thanks for asking." "San Francisco weather cheers me up." "I'm in love with San Francisco." "I'm very busy doing nothing."

My cheerful, lively young grandchildren came to visit. Everyone thought I was baby-sitting them. The truth was quite the opposite. As long as they were with me, they connected me to robust life.

I had trouble with the fact that my pronouns and verbs had to change. So many things in life had been *ours.* Our belongings, our theories, our writings, our therapy, our teaching. If I recognized that the therapy was still ours, then I'd stumble over verb tenses. It's our Redecision therapy, but we no longer teach it. I teach and Bob taught. Over and over, I'd change from present to past tense, and then be too sad to finish the sentence. Talking with a therapist friend I began, "One way we handle negative transference is..." and then I began to weep. He looked away, embarrassed, and I never managed to tell him what I'd been about to say. I think, Bob thought; I live, he lived. There was so much pain in simple grammar.

Time was skewed. When I chose a new physician in San Francisco, I couldn't give her a true history. I knew exactly when I'd had my tonsils out, when the whole family had scarlet fever and the bout with boils during my childhood. I knew when my children were born and when their diseases occurred, but I couldn't get my own recent past to fit together properly. I couldn't tell her what year I'd had my arterial bypass or when my diabetes started.

There was our time together when Bob lay dying, which seemed to have taken many years, and there was the time since February 12, which also seemed very long. When I got my charts from my Watsonville doctor, I didn't believe them. It wasn't possible that we were a normal, healthy couple—with Bob able to swim, walk beside me, and work—only three years before.

A friend, whose wife had been dead for ten years, told me his time sense of the years preceding his wife's death was still bizarre. This was one of his strangest reactions to her death.

It wasn't easy, but I was trying hard to cope with all this strangeness, and I'd had no past experience with such grief, no way to know how to handle it. No one has. I gave to beggars to assuage my guilt at not being actively involved in causes that were important to me. The problem was, I didn't have the inner strength to do more than exist on the surface of my life. I assumed that I was healing.

I kept reminding myself to appreciate the advantages of living alone. I could choose what I wanted to eat and when I wanted to eat it. I invented new mealtimes and sometimes snacked in bed at midnight. I didn't have to hear football games or music played at high volume. Both sides of the bed were mine. I didn't have to do anything for anyone. There were more advantages, but this was about as far as I ever got in my list of positives before becoming despondent.

I continued making lists of "shoulds." I should not deny myself fun. I should make new friends. I should not talk constantly about Bob. I should tell people what I think rather than what Bob would have said if he were here. I should choose my actions and not blame them on him. There should be no "Bob would want me to..." I should acknowledge that he was permanently dead and that I could live without him.

My daughter Karen reminded me that I had not had a dinner party since Bob died. She thought it would be good for me to invite friends to the apartment, and she offered to do the cooking if I didn't want to bother. After she fussed at me a while, I actually invited eight people one Friday night, including Karen and her partner, Robert. The next night I fixed dinner for ten. Afterward, I told myself that I'd never give another.

All in all, I believed I was functioning quite well. I was trying to prove to myself that I could manage widowhood in the healthiest and best possible way. I even thought I knew what that meant.

> *Dream: I am walking along the shore, and I see mounds of dead bodies covered with sand. Somehow I know which is Bob's body, and I dig frantically with both hands to get the sand off him. Suddenly he jumps to his feet and shakes off the remaining sand. "Poor baby," he says, just as he often did when I was upset about something. The words and tone are totally familiar, and I feel him holding me softly against his chest. "You thought I was dead. Well, I wasn't. Let me show you what I did." He points to a hole in the sand. "See, I scooped out the sand under my face so I could breathe. Pretty clever of me, huh?"*

Before I could respond, I woke up. He was still dead and I was sobbing.

Nae living man I'll love again,
Since that my lovely knight is slain;
Wi ae lock o' his yellow hair
I'll chain my heart for evermair.
—Anonymous, "The Lament of the Border Widow"

Men

Several of my widowed friends were dating, and I partly envied them. Dating would be a distraction from lonesomeness and carried a hope that someday I might heal. I liked being with men, but my friendships were just friendships. They were never dates.

Marvin, a psychotherapist from overseas, phoned that he would be in San Francisco overnight and invited me to dinner. I thought of the many conferences when he and his wife, Pat, and Bob and I were together, and I told him I'd be delighted.

He walked into my apartment, opened his arms very wide as I remembered him doing in the past, and smiled. "It's really good to see you, Mary." He didn't seem older, but it had only been about two years since the last time we were together. In those two years, both Pat and Bob had died. Marvin and I clung together and then separated silently.

"Good to see you, too," I told him, remembering in a painful flash that Bob always greeted him with, "Good to see you, old buddy," and pounded his back as they hugged. I didn't ask Marvin if he remembered, but I felt tearful. "I'm sorry about Pat."

"And Bob."

We went to an Italian restaurant just a block from my apartment. Through dinner, we talked mostly about therapy and therapists we both knew. Marvin still maintained a full practice.

"I can't retire. What would I do?"

"I go to movies, see friends like you, and read. I went to Costa Rica. Bob wouldn't retire, either, until he had to."

"Neither would Pat."

After dinner, we returned to my apartment and drank diet colas. Long ago, the four of us used to get drunk together. Now neither Marvin nor I drank.

He began to talk about Pat's death. "You know, she died so fast. Her doctor said she had three to nine months. Our friends told us about all the people they knew who were given three months and lived for years. We believed them. I thought we had time. If I'd only known, I'd have stopped working and been with her day and night. You and Bob were together all the time. I wish we'd had that, but I didn't know. Then she was in a coma. I was at work when they telephoned me from the hospital. She was brought in by ambulance in a coma, and she never recovered, just a month after the doctor gave her three months to a year." He wasn't crying. He wasn't the crying type. "We didn't even say good-bye. That's what gets to me the most."

I told him Bob and I had three years of knowing he was dying, and we didn't say good-bye. "I am sorry about that, too. I think about it lots—about how I'd do it if I could do it over. I'd insist on saying good-bye, even though he didn't want to. I'd thank him for everything."

"It's ironic, isn't it? We're experts. We've taught people how to say good-bye, and we didn't say good-bye." He added, "Maybe nobody does it right," and I agreed.

We continued to obsess, which was also ironic. We both knew that survivors needed to say good-bye after a death rather than concentrate their energies on futile wishing that something in the past could be changed. Here we were, two so-called experts, doing what all grieving humans do. We kept on mulling over little scraps of wishes to change the past. What we really wished was not that we had said good-bye. We wished our lovers were with us right that minute.

We talked on, with our memories creating two ghosts—Bob and Pat—who hovered between us. We remembered some of the good times together. Once the four of us went swimming in a hot, outdoor pool in Canada, while the snow swirled around us. Another year we attended a conference together in Switzerland, and later drove in the mountains and around the countryside. Marvin and I agreed on the usual irrelevant banality, that we'd been among the lucky people in this world, because we both had loved and been loved for many years. Then again, we spoke of our desires for better good-byes, better funerals, and more time before the deaths. We talked into the night about what we should have done. Then we kissed and he left.

Several months later, I learned that Marvin had a new, young lover. I wrote to congratulate him and wished him well. By return mail, he answered that it hadn't worked out. We kept writing, resurrecting the past and describing the present. That was all there would ever be between us.

I have one male friend, a psychiatrist, who didn't know Bob. During the early '60s before Bob and I met, he and I picketed together for civil rights and against the war in Vietnam. We also worked together. After twenty-five years of not seeing each other, we became friends again.

I admitted to myself that lunch with him was special. It was the only time I bothered to put on lipstick, even though he probably didn't notice. We usually sat together in the small park near my apartment—me with a salad and he with a sandwich purchased at the local deli—and we'd talk together, sharing opinions about the world. We were close, precisely because he had a wife he loved tremendously.

There were other men in my life. I often chatted with a homeless Black man who hung out near my apartment building. I admired his spirit in the face of his chronic failure to make an easier life for himself. He slept outside, refusing the local shelters because he hated having to sleep in crowded rooms with men who smelled and snored.

He told me, "I don't like asking for money for nothing." He put aside every nickel he could until he'd saved enough to buy a stool, footrest, and cans of shoe polish. He picked forbidden flowers to make his spot attractive, and opened for business. The trouble was, nobody wanted shines and—because he was now a businessman rather than a beggar—nobody flipped quarters his way. He tried to sell his shoeshine equipment, ended up giving it to another homeless person, and returned to begging. Then for a two-month period, he was gone.

When he came back, smiling as usual, he explained he'd gotten a warehouse job, but the place changed hands and closed down without paying the men for their final week of work. He got a ride to Los Angeles to visit his family, hoping life might be easier there, "But they was crazy!" So he came back here. He was my only dollar charity among the street people, and I usually paid up daily.

Just today there was a somewhat attractive man about my age in the elevator. I said, "Beautiful night."

"Colder than last night."

"That's true, but it's beautiful outside. The moon is full."

"That's when things get strange in San Francisco." He got off.

I wondered, if he had not made his weird comment, what weird comment I'd have made. Even when I initiated a greeting, I didn't really want it to lead to anything.

I received occasional visits from young male therapists who trained with Bob and me, and I always enjoyed them. The truth is, I especially liked men twenty years or more my junior; these visiting therapists; Carlos in Costa Rica; the strong, magnificently confident San Francisco cable car drivers; and any other men I saw on the streets of San Francisco. I felt especially close to my gay friends.

I went on being alone for the first time since I was twenty years old. In spite of my lists of the advantages of aloneness, it was hard not to be lonely. I understood why many widows were searching for a partner, in an attempt to abort the chronic ache of loss. But I didn't want a substitute for Bob. I wanted Bob only.

I treasured every dream of Bob, even the painful ones, and didn't want them to stop. I dreamed of Bob alive, comforting, tender, and bragging enthusiastically. Although I knew I was being irrational, I felt as if he came into my life in these dreams, to live for a bit longer with me. Of course, I invented the dreams. I could hear him saying, "Claim your own dreams," as he told participants in our therapy groups.

I claimed the dreams, and I wished I knew how to invent him into my dreams every night. Usually my dreams of Bob were quite simple. We were doing therapy together, or talking with friends, or nothing really seemed to be happening except that he was with me. During the dreams I didn't notice how wonderful, important, beautiful, and miraculous they were. For twenty-seven years before his death, he was with me, and these dreams were a reflection of that time. When I woke up, I would go over each dream, reliving it. I cherished them all. Sometimes I'd spend most of the morning just lying in bed redreaming the dreams of Bob, and I wouldn't even open my eyes.

> *Dream: Bob and I are sitting together on a couch somewhere, and I am showing him videos of the past year, to catch him up on everything that happened since his death. We are having the kind of quiet, good time that was typical for us when we were alone. With an audience, we often competed for attention, but alone our love was natural and relaxed. In the dream, we are laughing, enjoying the video, and having a fine time together. He is cuddling me, when suddenly a mutual friend jumps out of the video and says to me, "Come dance!" I refuse, saying, "I only dance with Bob." Then I wake up.*

Both Bob and I would have understood that dream. I never could dance. I am awkward and can't keep time to music, but during my adolescence and first marriage, I danced because I thought I had to. Bob solved this for me. He said I didn't have to dance if I didn't want to. He insisted that I was not awkward with him and, believing him, I relaxed. Sometimes at conferences or parties we danced together a bit, and I watched while he danced with others. When I was asked to dance, I always refused, just as in my dream. My rationale: If I agreed to dance with one friend, it would be impolite to refuse the next, and with most people I would feel awkward. Besides, I only wanted to dance with Bob.

The dream was about more than our dancing. Bob asked me several times during our lifetime together, "If you die before I do, may I marry again?" He explained in an almost guilty way. "I'm not like you. I could never live alone. It wouldn't have anything to do with you or how much I love you. Just say it's OK."

I told him it was OK. "You can do whatever you want. Why would you even ask? When I'm dead, I won't exist. There'll be no me to know or care what you do." I also told him that I would not marry again, and I knew he liked this. While asking for a special dispensation for himself, his silence about my decision was proof of his hope that I would stay true to him beyond his lifetime.

Through the years, he repeatedly said that we were different, that he knew I could live alone quite well. Just a few months before he died, he phoned the local jeweler and had their entire stock of wedding rings brought to the house. He picked a new one for me and said, "I wanted to buy the most expensive one they have, but I knew you'd have a fit." (He was right.) Though it wasn't the most expensive, he certainly didn't purchase it in order for me to toss it out after his funeral. I knew that he was saying, "Stay mine."

He didn't allow himself to imagine me with anyone else, in the same way that he refused to imagine his own death or imagine that he was dying, even when he wished aloud to die. That was why we never said good-bye.

I was not bound by what I believed to be his desire. The truth was, if I'd asked him directly, "When you are dead, may I dance, may I make love, may I marry?" he would have answered me in the same way I answered him. He believed in good-byes; they allowed people to free themselves to live wholeheartedly in the present. In his beautiful sanity and love for me, he wouldn't have wanted to bind me with his irrational pretense that we could always be together.

Bob no longer existed. He had no power over me. He was not responsible for the stubbornness I felt. I did not want anyone else, although I liked men. I turned on to men who were happily married, strangers, too young, or gay. I didn't turn on to anyone who might conceivably be available. My beautiful, desolate stubbornness irrationally supported what Bob irrationally wanted. I would not dance, live, or love with anyone else. Alive versus stubborn made an interesting impasse.

The greatest poverty is not to live
In a physical world, to feel that one's desire
Is too difficult to tell from despair.
—Wallace Stevens, "Esthétique du Mal"

Massage

I was asked to do a two-day institute for therapists at a transactional analysis conference in Cochin, India, and I turned that invitation into "one of Mary's many trips of a lifetime," as Bob used to call them. This time my daughter Karen, sister Bette, friends Ruth McClendon and Les Kadis, and I planned to attend the conference and then spend three weeks touring India. Afterward, my sister and I would continue to Sri Lanka, Singapore, Cambodia, and Bali.

It was almost twenty years since Bob and I traveled in India, and this time I brought with me my now-familiar "shoulds" and "should nots" to monitor my conduct. Do not compare this trip with my two India adventures with Bob. Do not talk incessantly about Bob and what he did, said, felt, liked, and hated. I should find new excitement and enrichment that had nothing to do with him.

I think I obeyed my rules fairly well, even though for me Bob was my constant, unseen companion as I showed my daughter many places he and I had loved. Karen's total joyousness sparked my own. I moved back and forth from sadness to excitement on a daily basis.

The therapists I taught were delighted with my ideas and vied with each other to be patients in my demonstration groups. I should have been pleased with my work, but I thought it was stilted. It didn't feel easy. I took little pleasure in their praise and began to grow tired of both my work and my unending *shoulds.*

After India, Bette and I went on to Sri Lanka. One day I was lying on a deck chair at a beach near Kalutara, looking out to sea and relaxing between swims. I was keenly feeling my mourning, and keeping my feelings to myself. I didn't want to grieve my way from country to country. Permitted or not, grief can grab ferociously and hang on even at a beautiful beach. On this long trip, I had stifled all sorrow, and was now suffering from physical tension caused by four stoic weeks.

As we sat together, a small old man approached, bowed slightly, and asked, "Massage, mesdames?"

My sister said, "No."

A massage was exactly what my tight body needed. I asked the price. It would be $3.50 in U.S. dollars. Even if I didn't feel the need, I'd never resist such a bargain. I nodded, stood up, and followed him. He led me to a shack at the edge of the beach. Inside, he said, "No suit." I took mine off and lay face down on the table, which was covered with clean towels.

He began by using his fingertips and the sides of his hands in split-second probing along the muscles of my back and buttocks. His method was more akin to shiatsu than to a European massage, but was also different. At first I didn't like it. My muscles were irritated rather than calmed. Then all irritation vanished, and I began to appreciate the skill and complexity of his hand movements. Each hand and every fingertip did something intrinsically special, and together they produced an exciting physical melody played into my skin and muscles.

He continued quick jabs with the tips of his fingers, while his palms and the sides of his hands swirled across my back and upper legs. My body began to feel invigorated, then vibrantly alive. His speed crescendoed, and my mind as well as my body let go.

He asked, "You like?"

"Yes. Very much."

His fingers worked more deeply, magically, while also still swirling lightly and rapidly over my skin. The sensation was sensual and then became sexual. I knew that before the massage was over, I would come to orgasm. And I knew that he knew.

"You like?" he asked again.

"Yes."

"Now front."

I turned over.

He never at any time touched my breasts or my genitals, and yet those parts didn't feel left out. He was bringing me to orgasm most expertly and in a way I had never before experienced. When I came, silently, eyes closed, he softly, softly moved his hands over my stomach, around my chest, down my legs, and over my face and head, and my orgasm followed his fingers everywhere.

When he was done, he left the shack, while I lay in luxury a bit, and then put on my swimming suit and walked slowly into the warm sea. I was relaxed, I was not grieving, and I was most grateful to him.

Later, when I was again on the deck chair, he returned. "Tomorrow, madame?" At that moment I wanted to tell my sister to fly on and leave me in Sri Lanka. I yearned for days of swimming and orgasms, and nights of mourning Bob. There was nothing incongruous in wanting both Bob and orgasms. If I wasn't on a schedule that included giving a workshop for therapists in Singapore, if I wasn't on my way to the highlight of our trip, Angkor Wat, I might have stayed. I told him, "Tomorrow I leave. So sorry."

"What time you leave?"

"Too early. Six. Early morning."

He nodded and walked off.

I was left with fantasies of bringing him to San Francisco, where he could make a fortune giving massages and teaching lovers how to use their hands as he used his. Then I put a period at the end of that experience.

I was now more understanding and charitable, knowing for the first time in my long life that respectful sex delivered without love, without even the pretense of a relationship, could be just what a human being needed.

Bette left me in Singapore to do my workshop and went on to meet her husband, Bill, in Jogjakarta. The first day of the workshop was February 13, the anniversary of Bob's death. I didn't mention it, and neither did any of the participants, although some of them, especially those who had read *Sweet Love Remembered,* must have known. I was aware that an unspoken issue like this was contratherapeutic in a workshop, but I couldn't bring myself to say anything about it. My excuse was being afraid I might cry, and it was unthinkable for me to cry about my own tragedy while leading a workshop. This seemed especially true here, where the therapists were Chinese, to whom I was a foreigner and stranger.

In the beginning I announced, "I say 'we' because Bob and I developed Redecision therapy. So whenever I say 'we,' I mean the two of us." I tripped over the past and present several times, using the present tense as if Bob were still alive, and I didn't dare to correct myself. If the participants noticed—and I am sure they did—they gave no indication.

Bob and I prided ourselves on being able to work well, no matter what was going on in our private lives. Bob particularly was disdainful of therapists who shared unsolved problems with their clients. It was all right to say, "I have been depressed in the past," but never, "I am depressed." He told our students, "If you need therapy, pay for it; don't ask your patients to provide it." Using this as an excuse for silence, I handled myself in the manner that both of us would expect of me. I was proud that I functioned as a therapist and teacher in spite of my widow's grammar problem and my intense unhappiness.

Almost twenty years before this workshop, Bob and I spent a

wonderful few days in Singapore. I planned a trip around the world and booked us into very special hotels at each stop. The special hotel in Singapore was Raffles, where Somerset Maugham drank his Singapore slings and wrote fine stories. When we arrived at the hotel late at night, we were told they had inadvertently rented the room I reserved. For no additional cost, they gave us the huge, royal suite on the top floor.

Throughout the workshop days I struggled to avoid my memories, and during long nights alone I remembered the magic of the old Raffles and wept. I couldn't believe this dull city, homogenized and modernized by the current dictator, was the place where Bob and I ate exotic food in outdoor markets, photographed the crowded Indian section, and loved together like royalty in that fine suite.

I tell you hopeless grief is passionless;
. . .
Most like a monumental statue set
In everlasting watch and moveless woe
—Elizabeth Barrett Browning, "Grief"

Bereft

All in all, it was a wonderful trip from India through Sri Lanka to Singapore, and then from Cambodia to Bali. I'd been to Bali twice with Bob. But this time with Bette and Bill, in addition to all the charm and excitement around Ubud, I discovered the best snorkeling I'd ever experienced, off the coast of northwest Bali. I loved the brilliant green coral, the temples, and the soft-spoken Balinese people. I thought my sorrow was lighter, that I was mending.

When I returned to San Francisco, I was overwhelmed with grief. I wasn't prepared for such distress. I thought of mourning as a linear process, like recuperation from an illness. "Every day in every way, I am healthier and healthier," was my expectation. And now, thirteen months after Bob's death, my world was smashed. I became submerged in grief. I felt worse than right after Bob's death, worse than at the Holiday Inn when my diabetes medicine was stolen, and worse than when I sobbed to Carlos.

San Francisco had lost its charm and even its color. The streets were drab, and the usually bright bay seemed darker and unappealing. I was trapped in a fog of misery. I walked the streets of San Francisco obsessively, hour after hour, and at night I couldn't remember where I'd been or what I'd seen. I was like a windup doll, veering mechanically this way and that, until I became unwound and collapsed face down on my bed. Day after day I alternated between frantic walks and immobility.

Although my calendar shows I continued to spend time with friends, I was emotionally isolated. I told no one of my unhappiness, even those who were very close to me. I was silent with widowed friends, who would have understood and offered help. Loneliness had nothing to do with being alone. Alone and with friends, loneliness was life without Bob.

I hid from myself the fact that I was profoundly depressed, ignoring signs I would have noticed in any client. I was waking almost every hour throughout the night and had great difficulty going back to sleep. I knew that this was a classic symptom of depression, but I didn't confront that fact. I was unceasingly exhausted from lack of sleep. Because I was awake so much, the nights seemed to go on forever, doubling the hours of despondency. I hated night and wanted to sleep around the clock I began taking sleeping pills, which gave me only a few hours of respite.

I also denied my depression by telling myself I didn't have certain classic, important symptoms. Although I scolded myself for overreacting, I acknowledged no true anger turned inward or any sense of worthlessness. Nor did I admit to hurting badly enough to call my unhappiness psychic agony. How could I think I was depressed when I was able to laugh and smile with friends and family?

Because a depressed state can consist of so many different levels and nuances of sadness and pain, each person's experience is unique. Even a therapist who specializes in diagnosing depression might not self-diagnose with accuracy. At night, alone in my apartment, I felt the numbing fog of daytime leave me, and I hurt with a dreadful clarity.

I had no compassion for my pain. More than a year had passed since Bob's death, so what the hell was wrong with me, anyway? As was typical of therapists, I was treating myself more harshly than I would ever treat a client, and that increased my despondency.

Sometimes I tried to comfort myself by imagining that I was talking with a therapist. Erving Polster, in La Jolla, phoned often after Bob's death and was especially compassionate. I fantasized flying to La Jolla to tell him, "I can't go on like this." I'd tell him how much I hurt. The fantasy was briefly comforting, but I didn't act on it. I was afraid that if I admitted my condition to anyone, I would fall into the abyss forever. I didn't even know what that meant to me. Depressed patients said, "If I let myself cry, I'll never stop crying," and now I found myself with the same belief. Although it was comforting to imagine therapy for myself, I told myself no one could actually ease my pain. Bob was dead, no therapist in the world could bring him back, and nothing else could help me.

A psychiatrist friend mentioned one of his clients, a widow for many years, who began her psychiatric sessions with, "Doctor, I know you think I'm crazy, but last night when I was talking with my husband, he told me..."

My friend said, "At first, I did think she was crazy, but now I think perhaps she was wise to console herself this way."

Although I neither could nor would believe in such conversations, I was very jealous of his patient. I mentioned to him that I was still strangely depressed, and he asked if I would consider trying Prozac. I didn't want it. He hugged me, said how sorry he was that I was grieving, and offered to help in any way he could. I said I'd let him know if there was anything I needed, but that I wasn't in too bad shape. Not true.

I continued to spend Thursday evenings in the writing group, but now, deep into my fog and pain, I wrote sketches of dead ancestors whom I cared nothing about. In this way I removed myself from anything personally meaningful, and got no relief at all. My Monday night suppers continued. Ruth and Les were intimate friends, so they couldn't be therapists for me, but their very presence gave me Monday nights off from depression.

Some families come closer in their sorrow, helping each other to mourn, but ours didn't. I saw Kelley and Kathleen, Bob's daughters, who kept me informed about their family. If they were hurting from Bob's death, they didn't mention it, and I didn't tell them how I felt.

My son loved Bob, so I could have talked with him. My daughters liked Bob, but were not particularly affected by his death. Their own father became ill and died a year before Bob died, and I had visited him several times with them. To some extent, we'd shared our sadness about his death, but it hadn't meant that much to me. Perhaps I avoided hearing their mourning, just as I was locking them out of mine.

I was so sad without Bob that I didn't know how to talk about it with them. Instead, I tried to be my old, cheerful self, and their very presence buoyed me up. It must be much harder for widows who have no family. Without my family, I think I might have chosen suicide. Their love and my imagined obligation to them kept me alive.

My daughter Claudia, a nurse, was chronically ill with lupus, and I worried constantly about her. In spite of her illness, she was cheerful on the telephone. I only knew it was affecting her when she'd say, "I was so lazy, I spent the whole day in bed." Then we'd discuss medications and whether or not a more stringent diet would help. How could I worry her about something as relatively minor as my chronic sadness, when her disease was threatening her life?

Mostly she'd tell me about her work. There was plenty of drama at the hospital, and her work stories were fascinating. Her phone calls also kept me in touch with the world of teenagers, as she recounted her children's doings. Ruth was twelve and Brian sixteen.

My son, David, phoned often, and we discussed politics. He also told me about his jobs and the doings of his two young children, John and Chandra. David often brought them to San Francisco to visit me. I took them swimming, and we played on the escalators; their hometown lacked such wonders. Chandra, who was only two when Bob died, would look at Bob's photograph and ask, "Are you still sad that your grandfather died? I am. He was a very nice grandfather for us, wasn't he?" I suppose he seemed so old when he was ill that she thought of him as everybody's grandfather.

My daughter Karen talked about her computer work and her home life with Robert. I thought of Karen as a dancer emotionally as well as in reality. She seemed to dance through life, with Robert as loving as Bob had been to me. I enjoyed talking with her, but our conversations often left me feeling more lonely and depressed than ever, simply because she and Robert were so happy together, and I was so alone.

After one of her phone calls, I rediagnosed my state. I was bereft. Though that was not a psychiatric diagnosis, it should have been. Love was gone and the world was empty. I said to myself over and over, "I am bereft. That is what is wrong with me."

It was time for me to fly to Mexico to do my annual workshop with Muriel James, a transactional analyst and author of many books, who had been a close friend for almost thirty years. Our last workshop together, sixteen months earlier, was the week before Bob died. I promised myself that I would ask Muriel for help, but when we arrived at Isla Mujeres, Muriel's husband, Ernie Brawley, suddenly became incapacitated with back pain. All her free time had to go to him, so I didn't mention my depression to her or to anyone.

As in Singapore, I worked well with the participants, and the only change that I could detect in my professional self was that I was more irritable. One participant was surly because the weather wasn't as nice as it should have been, and blamed me for picking April instead of February. When she talked about leaving the workshop before we were finished, I didn't urge her to stay, as I usually would have done. I was glad to have her gone.

I swam before, between, and after therapy sessions. The surf was a bit rough. For the first time in fifty years, I began to experience the desire to swim away forever. One summer during my adolescence, I had the urge to die by swimming far out in Georgian Bay, Canada. Looking back as an adult and therapist, I recognized how severely depressed I was during my adolescence. Then, as now, I told no one.

While swimming alone, I used the technique Bob and I developed in our work with suicidal patients; a time-limited, no-suicide agreement with myself. I would not let myself drown. No matter how depressed I felt, no matter how lonely, no matter how much I hurt, I would not kill myself accidentally or on purpose during this workshop. That meant I had to become my own lifeguard. I watched myself carefully to determine with each swim how to be absolutely safe in the ocean. I felt the same split I'd experienced at the Holiday Inn in Miami, when part of me collapsed, while the other part got the prescriptions filled and bought replacements for my mask and fins. This time the bereft part swam, and my inner lifeguard monitored the swimming. As I swam along the Garrafón Reef, over vast schools of circling fish, I was transported into a temporary enchantment and managed to escape my depression until the swim was over.

Returning to San Francisco, I made an appointment to see my physician. My diabetes was out of control. I wondered if this was caused by my bereft emotional state, but I said nothing about that to her. I did not mention being depressed. She prescribed a new type of insulin and changed the dosage of the old type. Then she told me that my latest mammogram, which was done before I left for Mexico, looked "spooky." I needed to see an oncologist immediately.

Instead, I left the country again. Nothing mattered, neither diabetes nor the possibility of cancer. I refused to consider extending my "no suicide" decision. I felt a kind of peacefulness settle inside me. If I had cancer, no one would fault me for committing suicide. My Isla Mujeres inner lifeguard stopped functioning.

When I left, I wasn't sure where I was going, except that I was expected at a South American conference in Brazil in a couple of months. My daughter Karen said wistfully, "If we don't know where you are, I suppose Robert and I will have to quit our jobs and just wander about the world looking for you."

I kicked around in Central and South America for six weeks, visiting Carlos and his family, and taking buses around parts of Ecuador. Then I went to the Latin America transactional analysis conference. There I began to feel better. For years I spoke with the Argentinian transactional analysts only through interpreters, and now I could talk with them and get to know them. I also had conversations with a group of Peruvian therapists, who worked with Indian children orphaned by the Senderos and the military.

I read my keynote speech in Spanish, but did therapy and explained the process with the help of Spanish and Portuguese interpreters. I received lavish praise from the young therapists, who had never seen Bob's and my Redecision therapy. They kept me working hard, day after day, and to some extent I came back to life.

From South America, I flew to North Carolina to attend the American Academy of Psychotherapists' (AAP) annual summer institute. On the plane, I became more and more depressed. I could almost chart the miles by my change in mood. It was as if a fog of sadness was creeping over me. Bob would have insisted that I take responsibility. "You are covering yourself with a fog," he'd have said. Of course, this was true. Furthermore, I was playing a lousy roulette game with the possibility of breast cancer.

A therapist who tries to cure herself can be like a lawyer who does her own legal work; both may have fools for clients. I decided to tell my friends at the Academy that I needed their help.

Give sorrow words: the grief that does not speak,
Whispers the oe'r-fraught heart, and bids it break
—William Shakespeare, Macbeth

Therapy

The first morning of the American Academy of Psychotherapy Summer Institute, my friend Irma Lee Shepherd said to me, "Let's have breakfast together." I looked frantically for others to join us as she steered me to a table for two.

"How are you?" She waited, with her calm, uncanny silence.

I don't remember what I said. I did not want to cry in public. The abyss was there, but so was she. Her presence made even an abyss feel safe. I think I told her, "Not so good." I don't remember what else, except that I cried, and she acted as if anything except tears would have been inappropriate.

At AAP institutes, therapists belong to leaderless therapy groups, called families, which meet together every summer. My good friends Irma Lee Shepherd, Joen Fagan, and David Hawkins were all members of my family. In previous years, I'd talked with the family about Bob's illness, but this was the first time since his death that I was with them.

I didn't ask for help easily. After Bob died, I fled all the way to Costa Rica to accept help from a stranger who couldn't even speak my native language. Although I'd been a therapist for many years, I was not used to asking for comfort or assistance.

I told the family of my bereft state. As the group worked with me, I heard myself say, "Bob took care of me," and knew immediately the importance of my words. Bereft meant "Bob is not taking care of me, and how can I exist without his care?"

In his healthy days and in his sick days, he helped me. Almost as soon as we met, Bob overcame my resistance to being dependent. He won me over with love, passion, and infinite caring. I had lived to age forty, doing for myself and others, while repressing my need for someone to take care of me. His caretaking was like a miracle.

As my therapist and supervisor, he cured my chronic depression in a couple of sessions. As my lover, he made me feel beautiful in spite of everything I believed to the contrary. He enriched my sex life. He taught me new therapy skills and encouraged me to write. His public relations skills made us a famous therapy team. I could at times be helpless and distraught, and he'd say, "Poor baby," and figure out what to do. He also took care of me by encouraging my natural independence. "Go do your traveling, Mary. I'll be here when you get back." His death was his betrayal. No wonder my depression hit so hard whenever I returned from overseas and had to realize again that he was not there waiting for me, that he did not exist. With the help of the group, I understood and mourned.

The next day I told them about the mammogram and my avoidance of the oncologist. Joen Fagan said, "The day you get back to San Francisco, what friend will you ask to go with you to the oncologist's office?"

Whoops! I wasn't ready for that question. I admitted how desperately I needed Bob to take care of me, but that didn't mean I was ready to let someone else step in. In my universe, there was no substitute for Bob. "My friends are as independent as I am. I can't ask anyone. My friends have jobs. They can't take off for my medical problem. I don't need them anyway, and there is probably nothing wrong with my stupid breast. I'd be embarrassed to ask anyone."

No matter what I said, Joen was adamant, and Irma backed her up; Joen firm, Irma loving, and both uncompromising. Sometime during this impasse, I called Joen a damned bitch for her absolutely perfect and true persistence. She heard me and didn't register even a change in facial expression.

I could feel the intensity of my resistance and could scarcely believe it. I told them, "I feel like a damn impossible patient," like someone other than myself. I was utterly stubborn. I refused to agree to be cared for by anyone except Bob. And then I heard the magic behind my resistance. If I needed Bob badly enough, he would come back. He would take care of me. I sobbed. Finally I admitted, "No matter what, no matter whether I see an oncologist or not, no matter whether I have cancer or a benign tumor or whatever, no matter anything, Bob will never come back. He'll never again take care of me." There was no magic for me. Bob's death was the truth and the tragedy in my life.

I told Joen, "I'll ask someone to go with me to the doctor's office." To get her off my back? No, for me. I figured out which friend I would ask and who the substitutes would be if the first friend wasn't available.

My depression lifted, and I mostly enjoyed the rest of the conference. At the final open session, I actually let tears show on my face as I told over three hundred therapists that I asked for and received invaluable help during this wonderful week.

When I returned to San Francisco, I was much happier than when I left. My diabetes was under control, and the biopsy of the lump in my breast did not turn up cancerous. I was sad sometimes, of course. A tune, a sight, anything might remind me of Bob, but I practiced telling friends I was sad instead of giving my usual "I'm OK" response. That helped me feel connected rather than isolated.

I received additional therapy, this time with a body therapist,

Don St. John. When Don phoned to tell me he'd be in San Francisco for three days, I immediately scheduled two sessions with him, as I always did. He worked on my body many times in the past, and when Bob was ill, he came to our institute to expand Bob's chest muscles so he could breathe more easily. Don did body work on my father when my father was ninety-two years old. None of us asked him for psychotherapy, although Don was a psychotherapist who combined both disciplines.

My only current body discomfort was occasional headaches, seemingly caused by tightness in my neck and jaw muscles. I asked Don to work on those areas, plus whatever else he found that needed his hands.

At the beginning of the first session, he worked with my neck and shoulders and then moved to my chest. As he massaged the muscles in my chest, I began to cry. I'd never cried with him before.

How many times did a person get to cry, anyway? I cried at the Holiday Inn at the airport. I cried with Carlos. I cried with my Academy family, and in front of all the people at the American Academy of Psychotherapists. Wasn't that enough? When did all this crying become self-indulgence? When would I knock it off? It was now a year and a half since Bob died. Who wanted to put up with blubbering? I couldn't stand it myself.

"What's going on?" Don asked.

"Oh, damn, I guess I'm sad."

Don increased the pressure that started my tears. "Let your body talk."

"I'm lonely, lonely, lonely."

"Let your body say more."

"I need to be touched. I am so lonely for touching."

Don continued silently, his hands pressing hard and stretching my tightness. I felt as if his hands were opening a vast pocket of grief inside me. He encouraged me to let myself scream. At first I made only sounds, and then the words, "I loved him, I loved him!" I exploded with grief.

Back in my apartment, I cried all evening. I turned my radio to top volume, so no one would hear me. As I screamed, I felt renewed. Implosion and sucking feelings in keep people half alive, without vitality, and with a depression that can become chronic. People are taught from childhood to implode, to hold everything inside. I knew from my experience at the AAP conference that explosions were good for me, so I didn't try to stop. As I screamed and sobbed, I began to feel my fury at Bob for killing himself with cigarettes.

We'd both been heavy smokers for years. When I stopped smoking more than fifteen years ago, he refused to quit, although his emphysema was already a problem. He continued chain smoking even while on oxygen. Once he burned his face badly, and still insisted on inhaling smoke and oxygen simultaneously.

During his lifetime, I was angry and frustrated about his smoking. After his death, I heard other therapists express their anger that he'd killed himself with cigarettes, but I let their words wash over me. I thought I was done with being angry for something that couldn't be changed. Now I screamed my fury. "You killed yourself! You could be here with me right now if you'd just stopped smoking. Why in hell did you cure everybody but yourself?"

Then I remembered, "You didn't take care of me all that well, either!" In 1987, when I was in the hospital having a bilateral aortic-femoral bypass, as awful a procedure as the name suggests, Bob was in terror that I might die. Although he stopped drinking several years earlier, he showed up in the intensive care unit absolutely drunk and so obnoxious that the nurses had to threaten to call the police in order to make him leave. "That's care, you son of a bitch. You drank; you smoked." I screamed and hollered, and by the end of the evening, my nose was stuffed up, my throat hurt, and I felt as if I had a terrible cold plus laryngitis.

In the morning I was fine. I lay in bed laughing at my previous night's fury about the hospital, as I remembered not only the hospital scenes but also the fact that Bob had not been the only one who ever took care of me. My parents had taken care of me. Children do not survive on their own. And even in the hospital during my terrible stay in intensive care, all three of my own adult children were with me, in spite of the staff's attempts to shoo them away. My daughter Claudia, a nurse, monitored the hospital care and made sure I got whatever I needed. I thought of Karen, who was furious at Bob for being drunk. After I was moved to a recovery floor, she said, "Why don't you divorce him?" I answered, "Because you can't divorce seventy-year-old men. It's against the law, I think."

Now I made myself coffee and continued laughing about my memories. Bob and I were a great team and a lot alike. We had fun, we lived life fully, and mostly we did take care of each other. We argued a lot, and other people often pitied one or the other of us, because of our quarrels and loud raging explosions. How silly those people were. Bob and I fought and loved, and in no way had our fighting diminished our loving. I began to realize that I now needed those fights. I'd been choked up and subdued through Bob's final months, and since his death I had no way to explode. I am a naturally noisy person as well as a tender one, and it was no good for me to stifle myself. I needed opportunities for screaming and also for outrage.

I walked three miles across San Francisco, in a blaze of sunshine, to the motel where Don was working. I told him about my crying and my anger and added, "I think I need to warn you that I don't know what will happen today." Was I warning him or me?

He said, "I'll consider myself warned." He pointed to two pillows on the bed beside the massage table and asked, "Want to pound them?"

I thought about it and felt no anger. I could tell that I wasn't holding back. "No. Not now. I've finished that part, although next time you come to the city, I might need some more yelling." I could yell with Don, and I could go out on a pier and pretend to be hailing people in a passing boat. I'd look for other opportunities for being loud.

I got onto the massage table, and Don began working inside my mouth, to loosen the muscles in my jaw. He said that there was little for him to do. Those muscles were much looser than they had been two days ago. I agreed. My screaming helped me physically, as well as emotionally. My whole body was more relaxed. Later, when Don touched my chest, I began to cry again, but this time my tears were gentle. I could talk as I wept. I talked of my desire and my unwillingness to seek a new love relationship.

He said, "You cry when I touch around your heart."

"My heart aches."

"Before you look for someone else, you're letting your heart heal?"

"I don't know. Even if I heal, there are no other men like Bob. You know that."

"Yes. He was larger than life."

After a while, Don asked, "Are you ready to say good-bye to him? You can do that here, if you're ready." I thought about it. "I can't. I can't do it, Don. It's crazy, but I can't say good-bye just yet." He wondered why that was, and immediately I knew.

I told Don that besides my memories, my nighttime dreams were all I had left of Bob. I was afraid, perhaps irrationally and perhaps not, that if I ever said good-bye, I'd lose my ability to see Bob in my dreams. "It's the only time I have him. When I am dreaming, he's alive. It feels as if he's alive. I can't give that up yet. I really can't." I was astounded at what I'd said, and knew I'd discovered a new, important piece of information for myself. I would not say good-bye until I was ready to give up my wish to live with Bob in my dreams.

After the session, my jaw was loose, my shoulders felt easy, and my neck was no longer squashed between head and shoulders. I was relaxed. Don and I held hands for a moment and then hugged. He said that he'd be back in San Francisco in December. "Perhaps by then I'll be ready to say good-bye," I told him, "and perhaps not." I felt tranquil and at peace.

I felt at peace for a month, and then crashed. The precipitating factor, as I used to write long ago in case histories, was a weekend leaderless workshop for psychotherapists. I hoped it would be like my Academy family. I invited two friends to join me, and we drove to the workshop together.

The meeting place was similar to Western Institute, but more isolated. It had a nice pool, hot tub, and beautiful yellowed hills with deer along the hiking paths. I fantasized Bob's reaction. "Drive two hours on a damned country road for this? A bunch of old cabins? Mary, our place had class. This is nothing." He said something similar about a place on the Russian River, where we once vacationed with a different group of therapists. I felt warmed by memories of his opinionated gruffness and his obvious love for our institute. He often said he'd never found any spot in the world that equaled Western Institute.

While I lay beside the pool, pretending to read, I let myself imagine that Bob and I were chatting together. While not as good as being with him in my dreams, it was nice.

That night at the first group meeting, I reported that I felt more peaceful than at any time since Bob died. I told them my recovery started with my work at the Academy summer workshop and continued with an emotional explosion during the session with Don.

Other participants told of their varied experiences during the past year, and also talked about what they wanted from the group during the three days we'd be together. A woman mentioned her fear of growing old. She wanted to come to terms with her aging process. Another said that was what she wanted, too. A man mentioned his relationship problems. Then I learned that a young woman in the group was terminally ill.

I had noted her slenderness at dinner, when she said she was trying to gain weight. I was ashamed that I paid little attention when she spoke. I now recognized that her thinness was a wasting process. I was horrified and grieved for her. She was so much younger than most of us and would not live to be an old woman.

I would always feel keenly sorry for anyone with her prognosis, but since Bob's death and my daughter Claudia's illness, I was so emotionally raw that I panicked in her presence. I wanted to gather her up, kiss her, and tell her, "I'm sorry for you. I'm sorry." I also wanted to run away as fast as I could. Selfishly, I didn't want reminders of what could happen to Claudia, what the worst case scenario could be.

A participant in the group began to use her own version of attack therapy. In the past I had tolerated attack therapy when used by staff and participants in drug treatment centers, but I never liked it. This therapist, in the name of honesty, began verbally abusing one of the older women, saying that the woman was disgusting. Her reasons were explicit and cruel. The older woman didn't defend herself and merely said, "I hear you," and "Thank you for being honest with me."

I considered the attack outrageous and totally unprovoked, and said so. The attacker suggested that she and I had obvious theoretical and personal issues to settle between us, and I disagreed. I was not interested in settling anything with her.

The following evening she told the terminally ill participant that she had never liked her, did not like her now, and considered her a freak. "You even look like a freak," she concluded. I was stunned.

The ill woman defended herself in a quiet, regal manner. Earlier in the day, I had talked with her and told her I liked and admired her. I repeated this now. Others became involved, and I withdrew.

I began to feel as if I were going crazy. I held myself very still, as I did long ago, when I was a sick child, and talked to no one. Images of Bob and my daughter Claudia kept flashing through my mind. Claudia had gained weight since her illness, and I thought it becoming. She didn't. Her face broadened from using steroids, and the telltale butterfly rash was often obvious across her chin and cheeks. I thought she was still very beautiful, but I knew that she was bothered by these changes. She was not at all a freak, but someday she might appear freakish to people such as this therapist. I began, very quietly, to weep.

Then I thought of Bob, as he appeared when he was dying. Because his mouth hurt for years, he hadn't brushed his teeth or gotten dental care, and had lost many teeth. The circles under his eyes were puffed and bruised. His skin was blotched everywhere and hung on his bones, while his chest was horribly enlarged from his struggle against emphysema. His face was flattened and swollen by steroids. He was once very handsome, and at the end I suppose he looked like a freak. I hadn't thought of him this way before.

As I sat silently in this awful group, I began to remember my own cruelties to Bob when he was dying. I'd loved him and cherished him, but at times I'd been cruel. Not like this woman, but cruel nevertheless. Once, when I was trying to clean him, I screamed at him, "I'm not a nurse! I can't stand this! I cannot do this for you!" I felt terrible, because he really was unable to clean himself.

Another time was late at night. He woke me, yelling loudly, "Oh, God; oh, God," over and over. I knew from his tone that he was not in pain and that he was doing what he often did, making noise so that I'd get up and be with him. He was lonely and probably both depressed and scared. I was very tired. I yelled back, "Stop shouting! If you want to talk to your God, whisper. I'm sleeping!" I'd wanted Bob to die, for his sake and for mine as well, I remembered painfully. As the group went on, I continued to damn myself.

Finally, I realized what I was doing, and began to wonder why I let this woman and this group trigger my attack against myself. So Bob had looked ugly when he died. So what? So I'd been impossible a few times with him. I loved him deeply, and I was proud of the fact that I took care of him tenderly almost all the time. He'd been thoughtful and loving most of the time with me, as well. Underneath all our interactions, good and bad, was love. Although I told myself we had truly been good to each other, I remained depressed.

The group ended Sunday at noon. During our drive home, the other two therapists in the car with me were discussing the attacker with anger. One of them, who once ran a school for dysfunctional children, said, "She's a chicken brain." She explained that whenever a child in her school attacked a weaker one, she'd tell the kids about chickens. "They pick with their beaks at any bleeding chicken until it dies. That's what chicken-brained people do, too." She told them, "No one is allowed to attend this school in order to learn to be a smarter or more skillful chicken brain. You are here to make your human brain more beautiful. If you want to be a chicken brain, go back to your old school for your education."

I liked what she said, but I couldn't shake my depression. That night, when Claudia reported by telephone that her new medicine was marvelous and she'd been pain-free all weekend, I still found myself morosely brooding about what new symptoms might develop in her future. I could not endure anything more happening to her.

I began to doubt that my love for Bob had been good enough. I doubted that my therapy at the summer conference and with Don St. John had been real. In some ways I felt more hopelessly depressed than previously, because now I began to believe nothing could help me. I believed that I accomplished nothing in all my grieving. I doubted that I'd ever recover or be happy. I didn't even think I deserved happiness.

I felt like a borderline patient, who, by definition, behaved exactly as I was behaving. When anything went wrong in life, borderline individuals immediately concluded that all past progress was a sham. After achieving some success, these patients were real dangers to themselves, falling into terrifying slumps when any slight setback occurred.

As I diagnosed myself borderline, I rebelled against this label. I was not and never had been a borderline. I was a fighter, and I was not going to let a chicken brain do me in. I would not stay bereft. I began to read through the journal I'd been keeping, to prove to myself that I was surviving in spite of this latest setback. All my happiness was not lost forever.

As I read, I learned something very important. Recovery was not linear. Its path was spiral. I had spiraled through despair, which I experienced many times, including when I lost my medicine at the airport; sadness that recurred whenever I was reminded of my loss; joy, which I felt when I looked out over the bay from my living room or laughed with family and friends; depression and the bereft state, as I told myself that there could never again be a home for me or a reason to live without Bob; fragility, such as I experienced at the weekend workshop; delight, when I traveled in new countries. Sometimes I ran the gamut of emotions in a single day. Sometimes I was stuck in my bereft state. Sometimes for days at a time I was happy. That's how it was.

My major task was to learn to be more patient with myself. As I circled or spiraled, I would love and accept myself. After deciding this, I had two dreams of Bob in quick succession.

> *Dream: Bob and I are sitting in a hospital waiting room, leading a therapy group of gay friends, some of whom in reality had died of AIDS. Bob is smiling and talking gently. He says to them, "Find joy each day."*

When I awoke, I cried a little but was also happy. I didn't explore the death aspects of the dream, treasuring his message instead. I tried to program myself to be back in the dream room with Bob as I went back to sleep. I wanted more messages from him.

> *Dream: I dream that we are sitting with friends. Everyone except Bob is in the background, shadowed. His face is lit as if by a spotlight. Gradually I notice that his photo taken on our wedding day, which I used on the cover of Sweet Love Remembered, is superimposed on his face. I wonder if this photograph is a mask or if he is wearing both faces simultaneously. I ask, "Honey, which is your face?" He doesn't answer and instead laughs his true, beautifully full laugh, and reaches out to me.*

When I awakened, I kept my eyes closed. I wanted to return to the dream. I could visualize his old, sick face and his photograph, but I couldn't hear his laugh. Finally, I got up. For the rest of the morning I was sad, believing that I had lost Bob's laugh. I hoped someday I'd hear it again in a dream. That was stupid. It was time to say good-bye.

As I started to berate myself, I remembered my rule that I would treat myself compassionately. I told myself that other widows were certain their husbands were watching them from heaven or hanging around as spirits. Some of them even talked to their dead. Since I couldn't give myself those beliefs, why not clutch at dreams?

I remembered that there were dozens of videos of our work. Just before the funeral, when I was in danger of throwing them away, a friend offered to keep the videos in her office. I had forgotten them. With those tapes, I could hear Bob's laugh again, and see his "faces" from our early work in the '70s until just a week before he died. I didn't have to wait for dreams.

As if to test this plan, the International Transactional Analysis office sent me a video with a Japanese voice-over for a Japanese friend who was visiting me. I suggested we play it, and he turned it on. I saw a younger, happy Bob speak his first sentence clearly before the Japanese words were overdubbed.

As soon as I saw Bob and heard his voice, I ran into my bedroom, sobbing hysterically. My friend turned off the TV and followed me, repeating, "I'm sorry, I'm sorry." I couldn't stop crying for a long time.

Obviously, I wasn't ready for the videos. Until I was, I'd take any dream I could get.

O Time! who know'st a lenient hand to lay
Softest on Sorrow's wound...
On thee I rest my only hope at last...
Yet ah! how much must that poor heart endure,
Which hopes from thee, and thee alone, a cure.
—William Lisle Bowles, "Influence of Time on Grief"

Time

As I became more accepting of my own emotions, I experienced a very calm period. The spiraling from happiness to grief to happiness slowed down. I wasn't joyous, but neither was I in pain. I didn't travel as much, nor read Spanish compulsively, nor did I clean frantically. I swam less often, was more relaxed about my hiking, and enjoyed being with friends. It seemed as if nothing special was happening, either happy or sad. I continued to hike in Golden Gate Park and walked alone through the city, carrying bags of sandwiches for the homeless. I warmed myself with their smiles and sometimes stood and talked with them. I missed Bob, just plain missed him, but felt a calmness, as if I were recuperating from a serious illness.

Too much of the time since Bob's death, I was walking through life slightly bent over emotionally, like a person recovering from severe abdominal surgery. I would become interested in friends, family, all manner of engrossing experiences, and then suddenly something would make me stumble just enough to feel the intense pain of my internal wound, and all my energy would be directed inward. With internal pain, it is hard to be interested in the world beyond oneself.

There were good times with friends, such as the Monday night dinners with Ruth and Les. After they'd seen their last patients, we'd start out, sometimes choosing a restaurant in advance and at other times simply walking until we felt like eating. When we managed to get ourselves completely lost, we frequently came upon new, exciting restaurants. Reiko True often came with us. She and I had started out in the therapy business together thirty years ago, at the mental health clinic in Oakland's county hospital, and we'd remained friends for many years.

Reiko and I visited Muriel James and her husband, Ernie Brawley, in Lafayette, to chat and swim lazily in their pool. Ernie's earlier back trouble turned out to be more serious than any of us had suspected, and he'd needed chemotherapy, but all was now well with him. He treated chemotherapy as if it was merely a temporary annoyance, and was eager to get back to his regular golf games. Quietly, I mourned for both of them.

One day Muriel and I went shopping together, and she persuaded me to buy a fancy new outfit for a conference in Florida, the first such clothes I'd purchased since Bob's death. After I brought it home, I didn't really like it, although I found many occasions for wearing it. I was dressing up more. I went to the theater with friends more often. I had many visitors. Life wasn't so bad. And whenever I was gloomy, I gave myself permission to grieve for as long as necessary.

I saw my family regularly, and that was lovely. I began to take pleasure in little things. One afternoon two tiny birds came to my balcony, whirring restlessly from railing to floor. I discovered a packet of breakfast cereal left over from the grandchildren's visit and sprinkled some of it on the cement for them, then carefully closed the glass door so as not to frighten them away. They squeaked nervously to each other, then, seemingly deciding I was safe, they landed on the balcony and began to eat. They were my first airborne visitors. There were hundreds of birds at our institute in Watsonville, and deer and skunks and coyotes and sometimes even a bobcat. I truly didn't miss Watsonville, although these birds reminded me of the times when Bob and I sat on the patio there and tossed crumbs to the birds.

While waiting for Western Institute to sell, I gave a few weekend workshops there for therapists who had been in our ongoing training program. I sensed an improvement in my work that pleased me. I seemed to be listening more creatively, and I took more time, refusing to act on my first quick fix-it impulses. I was startled by my own work, and didn't quite want to believe that inner suffering could make a positive difference.

I was no longer tired continuously. Perhaps during the years before Bob's death, I was more exhausted than I'd realized. His illness drained me, and I lost much of my spirit. Afterward, grief and depression were realities. Now I was experiencing tranquillity and creativity simultaneously.

During the weekends at Western Institute, memories of Bob permeated every session. Participants would say, "I was thinking of Bob just now," and then tell a favorite anecdote. Some of them trained with Bob and me for years, some joined the training program just prior to Bob's death, and all of them loved him very much. When someone used one of Bob's verboten words, such as "can't" or "try," the others would smile softly or weep as they remembered Bob shouting, "It's not *can't!* It's *won't!*" or ringing his loud "try" bell to remind them that trying and doing were quite different.

By now, all of the therapists in the group were experts in Redecision therapy and, in addition, brought their own exciting new ideas and techniques. These weekends were loving reunions; joyful, sad, and profoundly intimate. Bob's redwood tree was growing rapidly, a proof that time had indeed passed by since February 1992.

I went to Japan and worked twelve-hour days preparing a group of therapists for the transactional analysis examinations, the first to be held in that country. I returned without permitting myself to extend the trip beyond the two work weeks. For one thing, I decided to enjoy living in my apartment. For another, I could only afford to travel when I was paid. Wandering was expensive even though I combined travel and work.

As the months went by, Bob was less and less a part of my dream life, and I hated that. I tried everything I could think of to bring him back into my dreams. Before sleep and whenever I awoke at night, I'd relive times we were together and imagine new scenes I could dream about, but nothing brought him back. I even asked a hypnotherapist for help, but that wasn't successful. Not to dream of Bob was a desolation, a kind of second death. Finally, after months without dreams, I had a disturbing one.

> *Dream: It is evening, and Bob and I are in our Carmel office, where we worked together during the late sixties, before our marriage. We are both in his old black chair, and he is holding me on his lap. We are both dying. I am very, very thin, like a skeleton with skin over it, and I am very frail. This doesn't alarm me. I'm content, knowing I'll die in a few minutes, and then he will die. He doesn't speak at all. I tell him, "I can see bright lights ahead. Some people think bright lights mean heaven, but they are wrong. The lights are city lights. Death has no lights." He still doesn't speak, and that is unlike him. I say, "I hope you don't mind too much, my love, that death is black and nothing." He just keeps holding me, and I relax, imagining that he doesn't mind. People are beginning to crowd into our office, bringing fruit and beautifully wrapped presents for our funerals. I put my hands over my face, so as not to have to deal with these people, and Bob continues to hold me. I am engrossed in the physical sensations of being on his lap, being held by him, and I am completely willing to die.*

When I awoke, I was concerned about that dream and couldn't put it out of my mind. It felt like a dream from my bereft state.

I didn't like being so willing to die, and wasn't at all sure what that meant.

The dream also reiterated my belief that there was no life after death, that death was a void, and that I would not be with Bob after death. I had always accepted that and still did. Our only time together, in my dreams, was false, and I knew that too. My dreams were not real, but I wished I would invent more and happier ones.

I decided to let that dream remain mysterious, while I continued to monitor my health and enjoy whatever city lights I could find. I also determined that I had experienced a very beautiful life, and I could hold myself quietly, as Bob held me in my dream, when I reached a dying state.

In spite of my dream, time was healing my acute distress. I wasn't suicidal, was aching less, and even forgot Bob for hours at a time.

I drive my chariot up to the Eastern Gate;
From afar I see the graveyard north of the wall.
The white aspen how they murmur, murmur;
Pine and cypress flank the broad paths...
Man's life is like a sojourning,
His longevity lacks the firmness of stone and metal...
The dead are gone and with them we cannot converse.
The living are here and ought to have our love.
—Mei Sheng, "Years Vanish Like the Morning Dew"

Family

Today was a shining day, but it began in fear, because my daughter Claudia was coming to a San Francisco hospital for a test that couldn't be performed in her home area. My daughter Karen took off work to bring Claudia to the city, and I met them in the labyrinth of the hospital. When Claudia was escorted into the No Admittance Area, Karen and I got coffee and looked in nearby shops to find some sort of compensation-for-terrible-test present for her. When my children were young, I kept sickness presents on the top shelf of my closet, and whenever one of them had a fever, Karen would announce which present was requested. From the time she was barely two years old, she managed to climb onto that top shelf ahead of any illness, so she always knew every waiting sickness present. Now she and I were both anxious, and were handling our anxiety by shopping for Claudia.

Before we settled on a gift, Claudia appeared, breathless and laughing. She had passed the test. Nothing radically wrong was discovered. Right then we chose to ignore the fact that, no matter what the test results, she had had symptoms for some time, and they were getting worse. We decided to spend the day romping about the city, celebrating her victory in the laboratory.

We sat in a tiny, cheap restaurant at Embarcadero Center, giggling while Claudia and Karen ate $4.00 chicken-and-rice lunches, and I ate some uninteresting vegetables. Then we shopped. Everything went right for us. Amazingly, we all found shoes. Because we were cursed with feet wider and longer than shoemakers cared to accommodate, we rarely experienced happiness in shoe stores. "Bring out all your size ten wides, no matter what style or color," Claudia said. Karen could afford to be fussier, since she needed only size nine wide. We opened boxes madly, scattering them all over the floor. A woman said, "It looks as if a foot giant has been vomiting shoes everywhere." We laughed, exchanged boxes, and demanded more. The clerk found very fancy black boots which hurt my feet, but Claudia insisted they were just fine for her. I celebrated by buying bright green boots, which I may never wear anywhere.

Then we went clothes shopping, and we looked for Christmas presents for the kids. Claudia wanted to give her family a slot machine that took quarters, but decided it was too expensive. I bought one secretly for $150, knowing that the expense was absurd and delighting in that fact. I would give it to Claudia's family for Christmas. We laughed throughout the day from the pure joy of Claudia perhaps being less sick than we feared.

Bob's birthday, October 29, had come and gone, and I survived the day. Now the holiday season loomed ahead. Before Bob's death, Thanksgiving, Christmas, and Easter were times when our two families merged. He had seven children and I had three. Most of them came to the institute to celebrate every holiday, bringing their partners and their own children. During Bob's final Christmas, his entire family, including brother and sister-in-law, sons and daughters, their spouses, the grandchildren, plus my daughters, son, and their families all came to the institute. Everyone knew this was probably the last Christmas with Bob. He was too sick to tolerate the noise of so many people, so they took turns being with him.

It was also the last holiday when I saw all of the Gouldings. Last year, I spent Thanksgiving in Seattle with two of my sisters, three nieces, and their families. At Christmas, Bob's daughter Kelley invited my son, daughters, and myself, plus the Goulding family, and about half were there. This year no plans were being made for joint celebrations. I didn't quite know what to think about this.

Holidays at the institute before Bob died had not been a great joy for me. In fact, I dreaded them. I served food to the multitudes, while working around many people's schedules: Bob's ex-wife, our children's spouses and their parents, and the damned football and baseball games. My ex-husband and his wife cleverly decided, when they were first married, to celebrate all holidays a week early, so they weren't part of the grand scheduling snafus.

I always hated to cook, whatever the occasion. For too many years, I played martyr, managing family get-togethers because we had the only home big enough for everyone. I believed that family celebrations were one of the crosses, like menstruation and childbirth, that women had to bear.

This Thanksgiving, no one from the Goulding side of the family contacted me. I decided not to care, and didn't contact them. I knew I would never again be cooking for everyone, and I didn't blame anyone for avoiding that horrendous task. I could be bitter that family ties were being broken, or I could be thankful that I had a strong, lifelong relationship with my son, my daughters, and their families.

Karen and Robert invited me to spend Thanksgiving with them. I arrived at their apartment late that morning, bringing the ingredients and recipe for a very special stuffing. Karen made pies, and Robert had everything else ready to cook. Amid lots of laughter, the three of us stuffed the turkey, set the table with their beautiful Noritake china, and walked around the lake near their apartment while the turkey was roasting. When Robert's parents arrived, we had an amazingly peaceful dinner, because no children were invited. Then my son, David, his wife, Carol, and their young ones arrived for dessert. Johnny screeched his greetings as he entered, and the apartment shriveled to a size much too small to hold both him and us. He was pure energy, and reminded me of his Aunt Karen when she was six. Chandra, a quiet and sophisticated four-year-old, played with her toys and chatted with the adults. Claudia had been more like her. Then David and family drove me to San Francisco and spent the night with me.

Chandra and I were night owls whenever we got together. We propped ourselves up on pillows in my bed and read the entire *Mad about Madeline.* She recited all the phrases she had memorized, and especially liked to repeat firmly, "To the tiger in the zoo, Madeline just said, 'Pooh-pooh.'" As usual, before we finished, her parents and brother were asleep on the futons on the living room floor.

As I put away the book, she said, "That is our grandfather on your dresser." I collected all the photographs of Bob in the bedroom and brought them to the bed. Then I told her a story about Bob with each picture. "Here he is fishing. He waded into the cold water and cast his line and reeled in the fish. Do you know what that means?" I explained. "He is a very famous man, and here he's telling lots of people how to be happy. Here he is with all the family. And do you remember which one is you? You are the little baby on your mommy's lap. And here your grandfather is very old, and you used to come and visit him and ask him how he was feeling. Do you remember? And he'd say, 'There's my little granddaughter Chandra, come to visit me again!'"

She listened carefully, just as she listened to the tales of Madeline. Then she took her pillow to the living room and went to sleep.

I slept well, until I experienced a wild, early morning tremor. My bed shook violently, and I screamed myself awake, believing there was an earthquake. It was Johnny, jumping into bed with me. He was frightened by my fear, until I explained what I thought had happened. For the rest of the day, he was no longer my Johnny, and instead was Earthquake John. He loved it.

Later that morning Claudia and her children, Brian and Ruth, arrived at my apartment, and so did Karen, Robert, and his parents. Each family brought their leftover Thanksgiving food, and I added a pot of Costa Rican beans. We ate, went to the zoo, and walked downtown to see the Christmas decorations. That night Claudia and her children stayed with me. There was an advantage to having no extra bedroom and only three futons for the living room. I could entertain only one family each night.

We played a fine game with stones and a board, which Ruth bought with her baby-sitting money. Later, Brian gave me a résumé of the football season, because I ignored all professional sports since Bob's death. Brian knew vast amounts of esoteric football facts, just as his Uncle David had when he was seventeen. In the morning, Claudia and I watched Brian and Ruth ice skate at the new rink near my apartment.

After they left and I was alone again in my apartment, I felt a mixture of loneliness, peacefulness, and wonderment over beginning a new part of my life. The mix of emotions was bewildering.

During this Thanksgiving weekend, although I missed Bob and his family, I experienced a joyous déjà vu, a time warp. It felt as if this holiday came from a previous life, my life before Bob, when my children were young. There were the same friendly jokes, the excitement over new games, and the family closeness that was part of our early life together, when David, Karen, and Claudia were the ages of the grandchildren today, who were so very much like my kids of long ago.

It was all right that the Gouldings separated themselves from us. Perhaps they, too, were having holidays that resembled their youthful ones, before Bob and I tried to merge our quite different families.

On Sunday evening, Bob's daughter Kathleen phoned to tell me that she and her son, Daniel, went to Guadalajara for Thanksgiving, and that was why she hadn't phoned.

A week or two before Christmas, three of Bob's daughters came to San Francisco to spend a day with me, and we had a fine time.

We laughed, played with Kelley's new baby, went shopping nearby, and enjoyed carry-out Thai food, which we ate with my special chopsticks from Bali. I gave them Christmas presents for all the Gouldings.

I spent the Christmas season without the Goulding family. I visited friends and family in Watsonville for several days. On Christmas Eve, Claudia cooked a huge, traditional Christmas dinner, and after dinner we opened mounds of presents. Christmas morning Claudia went to work, and Karen, Robert, and I went off to watch Johnny and Chandra open more presents in their home. Throughout the holiday week, I hadn't been responsible for a single meal nor washed even one dish, and I'd never had a happier holiday.

I returned to San Francisco on Christmas afternoon for a spectacular hotel dinner with friends. This was first-class living! Then I returned to my apartment and started sobbing. I hadn't even known that I was sad. I cried for a long, long time and felt suicidal. I kept hearing myself ask, "How many more holidays must I tolerate without Bob?" I was being crazy, and I couldn't stop. For the next two days, as I opened Christmas cards, took phone calls, and tried to remember the joy I'd experienced with my family, I was back in the mysterious dream of our old Carmel office, on Bob's lap, wanting to die.

The dream wasn't all that mysterious, as I realized when I claimed both sides. I was the black hole in space, alone and hopeless. I was also the shining, exciting lights of the city. I accepted both parts of me.

Wednesday, I felt much better. My despondency was similar to a two-day flu—painful, but short-lived. This was the second Christmas without Bob. I was happy and I mourned. So what else was new? I wondered if it was time to say good-bye to Bob, even though my defiant opposition to that plan still felt like internal cement.

Here we walked when ferns were springing,
And through the mossy bank shot bud and blade:–
Here found in summer, when the birds were singing,
A green and pleasant shade.
'Twas here we loved in sunnier days and greener
—Robert Bridges, "Elegy"

Sale

The realtor's brochure reads: "As you drive up the dirt road to the Western Institute, you feel as if you are somewhere deep in the mountains instead of just a few miles east of Watsonville, California. There are redwood trees, pines, California live oaks, and blooming dogwood on both sides of the road. The property includes twenty acres of rolling hills covered with purple and white wildflowers and California poppies, a tiny private lake, and a grove of olive trees planted two centuries ago by Spanish settlers from Mexico. The trees are now wonderfully gnarled by time. There are many hiking trails. You can see deer, bobcats, squirrels, raccoons, and over fifty varieties of birds including hawks and owls. The ocean shimmers in the distance. The house is huge and impressive."

Finally there was a potential buyer for Western Institute. I was thrilled, and all day my eyes dripped tears. It truly meant the end of our era. That weekend an ongoing session for local therapists was meeting at the institute.

Whether or not the sale went through escrow, I decided this session would be our last time together on the mountain. I might come back alone to visit the redwood tree, and I would ask the new owners if I could place a small marker over Bob's ashes, but I would not work here again. This weekend I'd say good-bye to the property, and after that I'd consider saying good-bye to Bob.

Friday afternoon I sat alone on the patio and let myself remember. My first memory was almost twenty-five years ago, when Bob's brother and other Gouldings came to inspect the property. Bob, never a hiker, joyfully led us all on a tour and managed to guide us into the center of a vast field of poison oak. "Don't worry, keep going," he insisted. "The poison oak ends right ahead of you."

We discovered that the trail, but not the poison oak, ended at the base of a twenty-foot cliff. "Come on," he shouted, "You can climb it easily." Never before or since did I see him so agile. Later, as some of us drove to the local hospital's emergency room for cortisone to treat our flaring reactions to the poison oak, I recognized that Bob might have been wrong to deny the existence of the unconscious. Freud might have been right. Either Bob's unconscious directed that hike, or the devil made him do it.

Next I remembered the day Bob and I fixed picnic lunches, strapped them to our saddles, and set off alone on horseback. My daughter Claudia owned a brown horse, and Bob had just purchased a very large, all-white horse named Sinbad.

This ride was probably the dumbest thing we ever did in our lives. The brown horse deliberately went under low branches, rubbed me against the side of a tree, and then trotted much too fast. He paid no attention to my "Whoa!" Bob didn't have any better luck. "Sinbad is trying to kill me," he yelled.

We managed to turn the horses around and head them back the few yards to where our gardener was waiting for us. He removed the saddles, and we ate our sandwiches on the patio. We talked about the necessity of taking riding lessons, but never rode again. Whenever my three children, then in college, came to visit, they leaped bareback onto the horses, grasped the manes in their hands, and went racing up and down our hills. Workshop participants rode Sinbad more sedately. Occasionally one of them would persuade Bob to sit on Sinbad for a photo session.

Sinbad lived in the pasture with his best friend, a neighbor's pony, plus a couple of mules and some younger horses who pastured on our land. Dennis, our land manager, took care of them. Bob and the grandchildren fed them apples from our trees and carrots. Bob loved watching Sinbad run free, his white mane blowing in the wind. The two of them aged together. Toward the end, Sinbad took on the look of a bony ghost. He died a week before Bob's death.

For several years, we lived high above everyone in a cottage made of huge Norwegian Lincoln logs that arrived in a gigantic crate with every log numbered and lettered. After our children and friends helped us put it together, we moved in. In the early evening we sat alone on our porch, watching the sun set into the Pacific Ocean. Sometimes I persuaded Bob to listen while I read him romantic poems. His favorite was Lanier's "Evening Song":

"Look off, dear love, across the sallow sands
And mark yon meeting of the sun and sea,
How long they kiss in sight of all the lands.
Ah! Longer, longer we."

We were both romantics. We drank Manhattans together in those days, and were king and queen of the world. Sometimes, if we didn't have to go back to work in the evening, we'd sing. I couldn't carry even a tune as simple as "Twinkle Twinkle," but we'd usually start with that one because I could almost sing it. Then we'd advance to "Jesus Loves Me," and with another drink or two, we did duets of "Because," "Indian Love Song," and "Give Me Ten Men," all with wildly dramatic gestures and intonations. Then we'd hug and laugh our way to our waterbed. The cabin was our private love nest, but the amateurs hadn't put the roof on right, so when it rained, large drops dripped from the ceiling onto my face. For some odd reason, it never dripped on Bob's side of the bed. After a while, we moved back to the big house and rented the cabin to our land manager, Dennis, and his wife, Pat, who repaired the leaks.

Bob had many guns, but long before I met him, he'd given up killing animals, except gophers. Whenever he saw a gopher peering out from one of the millions of gopher holes in the side or backyard, he'd race for his rifle, shoot, and leave a large empty space in the ground where a gopher had been. I never saw him miss.

We were always buying things we wanted to like: badminton and croquet and horseshoe sets, Sinbad, drums, an easy-to-play organ, and a stupid electric car that never worked. We tried to enjoy them, failed, and then persuaded our trainees to use them. We lectured on the benefits of childlike activities, the value of fun in the life cycle, all while not really enjoying the toys we bought ourselves. We preferred to swim in our pool, sit quietly and look at the ocean far away, and stroll through our wonderful redwoods. Work was our major fun. Our joy was each other.

On our days off, only three days a month back then, we locked the lower gate, walking around naked in summer. We admired the roses, played in the swimming pool, kissed, sometimes made love in the shallow end, and never answered the phone.

If I could choose any life, I would choose the one I had. I wanted to do it all over, not to get it right, although certainly anyone could or should be able to live better the second time around. I wanted to live it again just to live it again, because we had a wonderful life.

More than four thousand therapists studied with us at "the mountain." Living with them, we supervised their work, taught theory, and were their therapists, while they analyzed our every move. We demonstrated our public personalities to them, our quirks, our opinions about everything, and we did it all with loud emphasis. No one could dare to claim credit for discovering what we were really like, because we told them unequivocally. Alone with each other, we were younger, softer, and less sure.

We were more genuine when we whispered in the dark. Our problems arose when we forgot this and believed that our on-stage selves were us.

Sitting on the patio, looking toward the ocean, I thought about those years, and told myself it was time to say good-bye to Western Institute. To do this, I shut my eyes and imagined all four thousand therapists massed together on our back lawn, spilling over onto the patio and down the long driveway on either side. Certain people stood out in my fantasy: the therapists who were our partners; those who remained good friends over many years; suicidal therapists who redecided to live and went on to create fine lives for themselves; the super-talented ones; the very few who remained perfectly awful; the therapist who first taught us how to use desensitization to cure phobias; the therapists Bob taught to swim; the therapists who worked in the prisons, in the slums of India, in the interracial district of downtown Los Angeles; therapists from almost every country in the free world. By now some of these therapists had left the psychotherapy field, and some, like Bob, were dead. Most were still working to help their clients change their lives.

I imagined all of them there in the large yard, waving, shouting greetings, and crying with me. I took my time, as I imagined speaking personally to many of them. Then I said, "Thank you for being a part of our lives. We gave each other so much." I'd see many of them in the future, but I told them, "Good-bye to our days at Western Institute. Good-bye for here, for now."

I let them fade slowly in my mind. The yard became empty. At first I pictured it as it was during our early years there, a thick green carpet of grass, and then I watched the grass shrivel as it did during the years of drought. I saw the earthquake cracks appear in the hard earth. I watched the tree surgeons remove Bob's favorite trees, the two huge black acacias, which, like Sinbad, were dying during Bob's last months. I pictured my son, David, putting in new paths, and gardeners planting native California shrubs. I saw Bob as I wheeled him down the path he'd designed, so he could have one last look at the new shrubs. He wasn't very interested, but he tried to pretend enthusiasm. By then he'd pulled away from the land he loved so much, and was concentrating his energy on the fight to get enough air into his sick lungs.

I said for both of us, "Good-bye home and institute. May you fare well." And then I stood up, walked past the redwood tree and the buried ashes, to my rented car, and drove to the motel where I was spending the night before the final workshop began. The next day I shared my memories with these very special therapists, who were in Bob's ongoing group with him until just three months before he died.

I hoped the new owners would love the property. They probably wouldn't shout at each other or drink Manhattans. I wished that sometimes they would forget, as we often did, to turn down the heat in the pool, and would wake up in the morning to find it so very warm that it was like a swimming pool in heaven—if there were a heaven with pools. Rather than fussing about wasting money overheating the pool, they would ease into the lovely water to swim together. I envisioned a couple who would someday embrace softly in the water's warmth.

Two weeks after that final workshop, before escrow closed, the group that planned to buy the property pulled out. They couldn't raise the money to purchase it. I was a bit frightened, because I would be without funds if the property didn't sell soon. I lowered the sale price, and hoped someone would buy it quickly.

We think of all the women hunting for themselves,
Turning and turning to each other with a driving
Need to learn to understand, to live in charity,
And above all to be used fully, to be giving
From wholeness, wholeness back to love's deep clarity.
—May Sarton, "My Sisters, O My Sisters"

Women

Closeness with women seemed easy for me in the days when my children were growing up. I had time for friendships then, and the women I knew were too occupied with raising children to analyze each other or need to parent anyone outside their own families.

My friend Velma worked the graveyard shift at the local telephone company, and we chatted for hours at a time. She connected callers to each other, while I, telephone propped against one ear, rocked David. Through the years, Velma was my authority on babies, because she had four of her own. By the time I had three children, Velma was working part-time and so was I.

On our days off, we packed picnic lunches to take to the banks of the Sacramento River, where we lay in the sun while our children made sand cakes, splashed each other, and swam in the water that we later learned was terribly polluted. I think she and I were happy together because we didn't intrude into emotional areas that might have been painful. I doubt if she knew I was often depressed. Perhaps she was, too, but I never asked. We didn't discuss feelings and weren't even aware that we avoided them. Together we had fun.

Rosemary, my second friend, worked for the local newspaper. Evenings, she and I ran off to campaign for Congressman Bob Condon's reelection. That was probably in 1954. We helped write campaign pamphlets, arranged fund-raising parties, and handled Condon's interesting assignment of asking his opponent nasty questions at the town meetings where they debated issues. Between political campaigns, Rosemary and other politically active friends came to my house to drink beer and talk long into the night.

I lost track of Velma when my husband and I moved. Rosemary and I remained best friends, as we attended graduate school, found new careers for ourselves, divorced our husbands, and married again—she to George and I to Bob. By then, our children were grown and had left home.

Bob, George, Rosemary, and I were very close. Part of the pleasantness in our relationship was that Rosemary and George disliked even the concept of psychotherapy, so Bob and I got a breather from our profession with them. We traveled together to Greece, Mexico, and Guatemala, and spent many weekends at their home or ours. Then Rosemary died of cancer, and later George did also. Bob and I mourned deeply.

We were friends with therapists all over the world, whom we saw at conferences and when we taught overseas, but as long as I had Bob, I felt no need for special friendships with women. Our lives were so crammed with work and workshop participants that in our nonworking hours all we wanted was to lock the gate and keep everyone else away. As another therapist said, "You two lived joined at the hip."

After many years apart, Velma moved nearby and we found each other again. Our friendship was as easy as it had been thirty years before. Both our husbands were dying, and yet we kept each other laughing. We talked on the phone, as we did long ago, and occasionally, when the men felt up to it, the four of us would get together. Velma and I talked nonstop, while her husband, Ed, listened quietly, and Bob laughed with us.

Every Tuesday Velma and I had what we called our "gripe luncheons." She began with a double martini while I sipped my diet cola. We talked in shorthand, using a word or phrase to remind us of an old friend or a long-past happening, as prisoners did when they yelled out a number or word to represent a joke that everyone in the cell block then enjoyed loudly.

Though we both were very much in love with our husbands, we insulted them gaily to each other. "So prissy Ed," she said, "hands me back his plate and tells me he sees a speck of something on its edge. I tell him to take off his damned glasses, and it won't bother him at all."

"I ask Bob if there is anything at all he'd like, as I walk right by his bed on my way to sit down and read. Of course, he wants nothing. But the minute I sit down, he asks me to hand him the telephone or the TV remote control, or bring him a sandwich, or how about turning on the light."

Those Tuesdays were safety valves, allowing us to blow off steam, away from our sick men. Toward the end, Velma and I acknowledged that we'd be widows soon, and even planned trips we'd take together when the men were dead. I had diabetes and Velma had a minor heart problem, but we didn't consider either important to our longevity. Just as when we were young women together, we never mentioned our sadness and pain.

One Tuesday during lunch, Velma told me that she was on her way to her physician's office for some sort of heart test. She assured us both that the test was nothing. That afternoon, as the test was being monitored, she died of a heart attack, although they kept her body alive two more days. Velma's husband died a few weeks after she did. Bob lived another year.

After Bob died and I moved to San Francisco, I was estranged from everyone, and that seemed natural. There was nothing in my life except the hugeness of my loss. When I began to want friends, I found that I was most at ease with couples who had been Bob's and my friends for a long time. Still, I needed women friends.

The very process of getting close to women caused me internal turmoil. At first, I blamed my difficulties on Velma's and Rosemary's deaths. If I got too close to someone, I risked the suffering that I would feel with yet another death. As soon as I recognized this, I remembered that Bob and I used to tell clients, "The only person you can guarantee will be with you for the rest of your life is you." I needed friends, and I would risk eventual loss to have them with me now.

My problems continued. I made new friends, but our contacts left me tense and angry. I became guarded, reaching out tentatively and then pulling back. I looked more carefully at what was going on and recognized that my early hang-ups with my mother had surfaced once again. Perhaps because I was a widow, women were insisting on taking care of me, and their ways of caring felt too close to my mother's ways.

I told one of my new friends about my decision to fire my dentist in order to save money. The next week she tried to give me $1,000 to rehire the dentist. Previously, she told me about her own lack of money and the difficulties she was having saving for her own old age. I knew her assets were less than mine. I should have responded to the love implicit in her offer. Instead, I could scarcely stifle my fury.

Throughout my childhood, my mother had wanted a fur coat, but each time she almost had the money saved for it, she felt compelled to spend it on our doctor bills, music lessons, or something else we didn't necessarily want. Her self-sacrifices were continuous and awful. When my friend offered money for a dentist, I felt like a cornered eight-year-old, trying to explain that I could afford a dentist when I decided I needed one. The friend didn't listen. My mother would not have listened either. That was the intolerable part. I heard myself scream, as I had to my mother in the past, "Don't think for me!" My friend, like my mother, let me know how much my anger hurt her.

Another friend treated me to a luncheon at a fancy San Francisco restaurant. As we were eating, I told her that Bob and I never ate there, because in the anti-hippie days the restaurant had a policy of excluding men whose hair was long enough to touch their coat collars. Bob's hair disqualified us. She replied, "Your marriage was dysfunctional," and began to diagnose Bob's pathology. I told her, "I bloomed with Bob's love." She continued to give me her unwanted opinions. I told her to shut up, and she began to weep. I left. Scratch one more friend.

A third friend explained that my current sadness would be relieved if I involved myself in charity work. She suggested I volunteer to work in the office of one of our favorite charities, where she spent several hours a day, and insisted it was selfish of me to stay home when I could be serving humanity. She was right; it would be splendid of me to become an unpaid, senior citizen file clerk, like other dedicated old people. But why should I scrap my own talents in favor of such a job? I felt guilty as I refused. She meant well, and she was voicing the beliefs of my own self-damning conscience. As long as I was in the city "doing nothing," as my friend said, my excuses for not doing charitable work sounded idiotic and selfish to me. I tried to explain my refusal to do charitable work with her, and she felt that I was insulting both her and the charity. I stopped seeing her.

I began to wonder if I had the capacity to like women. I wondered if I would ever let down my barriers enough to welcome other women into my soul. If any woman really knew me, I wondered if she could like me.

Mother loved me invasively, and I fought desperately against her intrusions. I insulted her often, yelling, "You don't understand!" or "You never listen!" while refusing to give her anything important to listen to or understand.

When I was in first grade, my mother returned from a school conference to tell me sadly, "Your teacher says no one likes you." "It's not true," I maintained with angry stubbornness, because it was so terribly, painfully true, and because my mother suffered whenever I failed in any way. I already knew at that young age that my unpopularity would be, in my mother's mind, her failure, her pain. The fact that neither of us had a clue as to how to solve my unpopularity problem would simply compound Mother's anguish. I had to wear armor; I had to lie. I had to do whatever was necessary to avoid revealing any of my imperfections. My hurts were inextricably entangled with her own. When Mother made my hurts hers, she kept them forever, telling me of them for years and leaving me both angry and perpetually guilty. When I expressed my anger, she was doubly wounded. Wanting friends, I wondered if I had returned to the unpopularity of my young years.

I simply couldn't deal with women who, professing love, mothered me as my mother had, gave me advice, and then refused to listen when I asked them to back off. Married women, who were still professionally employed, hadn't done this with me.

Was loneliness the problem that caused women to behave as these new friends did? Did women instinctively mother their children and their lovers and then, when death left them single and alone, did they automatically need to diagnose, offer gifts, tell others how to live their lives? Was it a female weakness to keep on mothering forever? I didn't want even the most positive mothering. I wanted friends who gave me distance, respecting their boundaries and mine, even though that might perpetuate my loneliness.

Most of the psychotherapists I knew, male and female, refused to retire. I began to understand. Through our patients, we received love, admiration, attention, and a kind of closeness, knowing their souls while keeping ours well hidden. As long as we had patients, we believed we had intimacy, and the search for close friends could be avoided. That was sad, I decided. I would continue my quest to find the intimacy with women friends that I had already experienced with some of the men in my life.

I signed up for a leaderless workshop for professional women in the mental health field at my favorite hotel in Isla Mujeres, Mexico. The participants ranged from thirty-five to seventy-four years old. Eleven women lived alone, including four whose partners had recently died. Six lived with partners who were not attending the workshop, and two were a couple. Workshop participation was by invitation, so initially everyone knew someone and no one knew everyone.

Each morning we met together for at least three hours. Small groups sometimes met for additional sessions during afternoons or evenings. We sat together in a circle on white plastic chairs in an otherwise bare room, surrounded by heat and the clack of ceiling fans. From the first day, we talked about what really mattered in our lives.

One woman described her move to Southern California. "We live in paradise, and I ought to be happy about it. I want to understand what's going on with me that I'm not always happy." She laughed, acknowledging that perpetual bliss might not be a part of the human condition. "Cross out 'always.' What am I doing to deny myself happiness?"

I mentioned my problem with anger toward women who tried to help me. Someone said, "I'm always into trying to help. If I bug you here, just tell me to buzz off." I felt instant relief.

A young internist said, "I'm burned out. I have a lot of older patients, and they don't listen to me. Maybe some of you can tell me what's wrong. What should I do so they'll listen to what I tell them?" We older women who had ignored our physicians looked at each other and smiled a bit guiltily, but had no advice to offer.

After a while, someone said, "I used to have answers, but there are so few things I am sure of any more." I remembered how powerful it felt to be sure. "I'd love to be sure again. Right after Bob and I wrote *Not to Worry*, the ceiling fell in on us." Immediately after the book was published, Bob began to have bouts of pneumonia and his emphysema became incapacitating, so I was continuously worried about him.

Older women talked about fears. The persistent but manageable fear of falling that made us walk cautiously, not daring to jump down the stairs to the beach. The fear of old age's real calamities: a stroke that could leave us physically helpless or even institutionalized for years; cancer; being widowed (for those whose loves were still alive).

"My husband and I talk about death. He's eighty-two. I don't know if talking about it helps." Those of us who were widowed could not come up with anything that helped.

We mentioned our worries that forgetfulness meant impending senility, and then began laughing joyously whenever one of us forgot a name or where she had put her room key. "Thank you, thank you," we cheered, because another person's forgetfulness made the problem banal rather than frightening, especially when the forgetful one was a younger member of the group.

Someone kicked over a glass of water, leaving a round, bright puddle directly under another woman's chair. It looked exactly like urine. We regaled each other with horror stories of wetting our pants when we were children, and decided bravely that we would not be traumatized if we began to piddle publicly due to age or infirmity.

Some participants brought small, happy gifts for everyone. On the first day, one woman announced her birthday was near, and she presented each of us with a pen inscribed with her name and birth date. A participant from Mexico said a piñata was just too large to load onto a plane, so instead she prepared a little packet for each of us with a miniature Mexican flag, serape, sombrero, and Mexican candy. Another woman found colored postcards of the snorkeling site at our hotel and gave one to each person. From time to time, someone left Balinese-like offerings of hibiscus and other native blossoms on palm leaves beside our bedroom doors.

The real gift from every woman was herself. We didn't solve each other's problems, although it was a solution of sorts just to be enjoyed and understood. We opened ourselves, our thoughts, our emotions, and our yearnings, and people listened with respect. A woman told of the pain of having to hide her lesbian loving through her entire professional life. She and her partner never dared hold hands in public or give each other quick, impulsive kisses.

A lot of pain was aired. A woman sobbed, telling of her divorce. Three of us spoke of our ill daughters. One woman had lost a son. Two had suffered childhood abuse. One had recently been raped and beaten. One was going blind and decided courageously to keep on living anyway. "I'm already listening to talking books," she said.

We shared our loneliness. A woman who was a widow for many years began, "I live alone. I have no partner, no family, and no living relatives. I feel an emptiness, where love is missing." Listening to each other, many of us wept, and learned that when we wept together, we were not lonely.

The women without families spoke of their concerns for the future. They had taken care of mothers and fathers. Who would care for them? One woman decided to ask a special friend, a younger woman, to be a daughter to her. Some liked the idea of establishing a group home in order to live with friends, and not be victims of managed care. They wanted a home where women appreciated each other—a home with the spirit of this week together.

We played. We splashed and swam. Two of us gave snorkeling lessons to anyone who wanted them. The fish were magnificent, and the water so clear that sometimes it felt as if we could see forever. One woman, thin and not a strong swimmer, rented a life vest for the week and bobbed everywhere, watching the fish. Another, with one fin missing and a mask full of water, pulled off her mask to declare, "This is almost as much fun as going to the dentist, thank you very much." Another sat like a queen on a deck chair, grandly giving the finger to anyone who urged her to get into the water. Four of us swam constantly, whenever we weren't in a meeting. Two women spent their spare time playing with and feeding stray dogs. At night, some naked and some not, we lay in the sand or floated on the soft, warm, starlit sea.

One day we talked about sex. One woman said, "I have only had sex with one person. We were married fifty-two years. A few months after he died, one of his good friends, a widower, asked me if I would like to go to Europe with him on the Queen Elizabeth. I just couldn't do it. And now, to tell the truth, I've thought of getting in touch with him to see if he is still available. But I'm embarrassed. I'm kind of like a virgin, if you know what I mean."

Another woman told us, "I've had several lovers since my husband died. A considerably younger man was my partner for two years. At first it was all right, and then it became a problem for me. He began to borrow money from me, and we both knew he'd never pay it back. I felt as if I were paying him for sex. I wanted equality in our relationship and it wasn't possible, so I stopped being with him. A year later, he came over and wanted to start it up again, but I refused. It wasn't right for me."

"The best relationship I ever had," said one of the divorced women, "was with a man much younger than myself. We had good years together, and then he left to do the things I'd already done—marry and have a family. I wasn't hurt personally. I knew from the beginning that ours was a temporary love, but I mourned. And I remember him with love."

I was surprised to learn that most of the unattached women rarely had sex, including the young ones. They weren't actively seeking lovers, although all but one expressed an openness for a future love relationship. No one considered my wish for sex without love or commitment to be inappropriate. In this group we accepted each other, and that was the richness of each day together.

We talked of our bodies; we old ladies didn't much like ours. We were too skinny or too fat, and either way we sagged. We joked about plastic surgery, but only one of us had a face lift.

Someone added, "I've lost my pubic hair."

"I didn't know that happened," said another. "I never even saw mine fall out. One day I looked down, and I was almost bare. I hate it."

"My pubic hair and my breasts proved I had become a woman. When I was a teenager, I was so proud of them. My pubic hair was soft and curly and lighter than the hair on my head. I used to lock the bathroom door and stand on the edge of the tub to look in the mirror at myself naked. Now my breasts are empty bags, and I have only a few scraggly pubic hairs. They aren't even curly any more. I wonder, am I still a woman or have I become a fat-stomached, sexless little girl?"

That night four of us sat in the sand together, our foreheads touching, cradling each other in our arms, as one would cradle a wounded child. Here we were—successful, even renowned, psychotherapists—mourning the loss of pubic hair. Then other women joined us, and we sang and danced together.

That was how we spent our seven days; laughing, weeping, playing, comforting, and listening. I found myself wishing and imagining that women everywhere, all over the world, waiting in line to fill their water pots, sitting together picking lice from their children's hair, cooking together or weaving or sunning on the front porch on a Sunday afternoon, were sharing their lives as we shared ours. We decided to meet again next year in Mexico, and support each other, by phone and letter, in between.

Heart! We will forget him!
You and I, to-night!
You may forget the warmth he gave,
I will forget the light.

When you have done, pray tell me,
That I my thoughts may dim;
Haste! lest while you're lagging,
I may remember him!
—Emily Dickinson,
"Heart! We Will Forget Him!"

Other Men

Although I hadn't yet let myself say good-bye to Bob, I took off my wedding ring. It was no longer comforting to pretend to the world that I was married, when I'd been single for two years. I continued to cherish as many male friends as I could find. I liked pen pals, swimming partners, visitors looking for a guided tour of San Francisco, and buddies who came for lunch or just to chat. I tried to be endlessly, nonsexually seductive, because I couldn't imagine a good world without male voices nearby. I was fortunate that so many people who knew Bob and me passed through San Francisco.

My body got more and more lonely. I wondered whether it could be acceptable to have friendly, uncommitted sex, when a person doesn't want romantic love. Can an old lady in today's world, who totally missed out on the sexual promiscuity of the seventies, try to recreate that era for herself, with greater caution against sexually transmitted diseases? As I had mentioned in the women's workshop, the "old lady" was me.

When I learned that a particularly good friend would be attending a conference where I was a speaker, I began to fantasize having sex with him there. I let myself enjoy the idea. He lived far enough from California that I rarely saw him more than once a year. He was divorced and lived alone. We liked each other very much. For four weeks, I warmed myself with fantasies.

How to let him know? I might say, "I haven't had sex since..." or "I'd like to have sex." Perhaps I might say, "Believe me, I am not in love with you, but..." or "Would you like a brief affair, just during this conference?" Critiquing these openers, I didn't find them very enticing.

Since I rarely chose my words in advance, even when I gave lectures to large groups of therapists, I decided not to worry about what I would say. When the time came, I'd know. My fantasies of our affair-to-be were lovely and guilt free.

In my imagination I dealt with any possible chagrin I might feel if this man said, "No." If he refused, he'd be making a statement about himself, his desires, and his preferences. His preferences did not define my worth. If he didn't want sex with me, I would be frustrated, and that was all.

Somewhere in the midst of my fantasies, I began worrying about the long list of sexually transmitted diseases. I went back to wondering what I could say, this time about safe sex. Do people ask each other, "Have you had any sexual partners within the last fifteen years who might have been exposed to AIDS?" or "Do you have herpes?" or "What else might you be transmitting?" How does one achieve the illusion of romantic spontaneity and avoid sounding accusatory or paranoid while solving the protection problem?

Nothing in my entire lifetime prepared me for what I was planning. With Dave, my first husband, World War II was ending and everyone who had not married during that war was racing to marry as soon as possible. The boys were coming back, and no girl wanted to be left out. My husband-to-be and I kissed on the first date, necked on the second, and he asked me to marry him on the third. I believed he had saved my life. In three months I would graduate from college and I needed, above all else, to escape the stigma of attending my graduation without an engagement ring. His proposal rescued me from old maid status. I graduated, and we married when I was twenty years old. The scenes I remembered with Dave gave no hints of how to behave today.

My two very brief affairs in my long lifetime had almost faded from my memory, and I simply did not recall how they began or who arranged what. I got no help from my memory of scenes with Bob. Bob and I worked together, grew passionate together, and I certainly didn't need to ask him for sex. At sixty-nine, I was a novice at instigating an affair. I never before even contemplated asking bluntly for friendly sex.

On the first day of the conference, my fantasy lover and I met by chance at the check-in counter and embraced enthusiastically. I spent the first evening in his room with half a dozen others. We partied and talked shop. He obviously had no lover here, and he spoke of none at home. We were working very hard at the conference, and our evenings were full. Fortunately, we were both staying at the hotel an extra night, so I decided to wait until then to approach him, when our friends would be gone. I considered this cowardly on my part, but decided that it was the best approach.

We had dinner together that last night, and then I went with him to his room for our usual good night drink. When I got there, I was still dithering about how to say what I wanted. I decided to begin with, "I'd like to have sex with you. What do you think?" First I said, "Tonight I feel like celebrating. I'll have a bourbon with you." Until then, I'd been partying with diet colas.

He put ice in the glass, poured bourbon over it, and grinned as he handed it to me. "Here's to you," he said. We clinked glasses. I took a long, deep breath before tasting it. I found the fragrance of fine bourbon lovelier than wine, neither of which I drank anymore. I sipped and wondered what I was trying to do—fall drunkenly into bed with him?

We rehashed the conference, laughing and joking about it. He imitated one of the pompous speakers, and I played a dull, pedantic member of the audience, asking incomprehensible questions which he answered with delightful absurdity. We were thoroughly enjoying each other. Now was the time to say, "Hey, let's have sex together." At that moment it would have been simple to ask. Instead, amazed, I heard myself saying, "Remember the time when Bob and you and I..." He remembered.

I couldn't believe myself. After mentioning Bob, how would I possibly move toward sex? I continued sipping the bourbon, and decided that I could and should be honest with him. I should say, "I'm nervous and I'm talking about Bob, because I'm afraid to tell you that I would like to have sex with you. I don't know how to proposition you. I don't seem to know how to flirt seriously." We went on talking about Bob.

Panicked by my own dim-wittedness, I wanted to say, "Wait right here in your room for five minutes, and I'll be back." I could rush to my room, phone one of my daughters or one of my friends who knows how to have an affair, and ask, "What do I do now? Please, tell me exactly what to do and I'll do it."

I didn't leave. He and I began talking about a new form of therapy that was discussed in a seminar that morning. As he talked, he put his hand, quite naturally, on my arm.

I could *do* something. Touch him—something. It didn't have to be words, I recalled from my long-ago youth. But if I touched him suggestively, he might be shocked and conclude that I was drunk. I might wreck our friendship. Besides, he probably had no condoms. For a month, planning this evening, I was sexually ready, and now, nothing. His hand did not stir me. What if I offered, he accepted, and I remained as dead and dry as I was at that moment? It was a likely outcome.

I had a second tiny drink, perhaps a tablespoon of bourbon, as we chatted on. I felt as if I were thirteen. I couldn't have managed this scene then, and I couldn't now. I needed my friends, my own grown children, someone to tell me how you get into the bed.

I said aloud to myself, "Should I have another drink? No, a glass of water." He got a clean glass, and poured water over ice. I examined the glass of water, sniffed it, and joked, "Somehow this fails to have the attractiveness of my last drink." I drank it down. "In fact, it was quite flat." We talked a few more minutes, I said good night, kissed his cheek, and took the elevator to my room.

A month of fantasies went down the drain. Well, I could always proposition him next year. Maybe next time I'd simply meet him at the front desk and whisper in his ear, "I want to have sex." I laughed at myself and wondered what I was feeling. Sad? No. Disappointed? Not really. I marched down the list of emotions, and came up with rueful, a word that described the feelings of unmarried, fictional women of two centuries ago, who hoped that dropping a handkerchief might lead to a romance that never happened because the handkerchief was never dropped. I went to bed.

I didn't want love, and I didn't want romance, but I did want sex. Then suddenly, without any advance planning, I took the first step. I asked, out loud and clearly, for sex. I propositioned a friend.

We were in my apartment. I said, "I'd like to have sex with you, just friend with friend. No love and no commitment. Are you available for that kind of sex?" He declined, saying, "I couldn't do that." When I asked why, he said, "I'm too conventional."

We talked about my desires and his reluctance. Even without sex, our evening was emotionally intimate, and I think we were both satisfied that we'd established a loving relationship and would continue in that fashion.

Afterward I was only a bit shocked at myself, and the shock had a giggling, happy aspect to it. I didn't berate myself. Some day I might find a male friend whose beliefs and desires coincided with mine, although I doubted it. It would have to be someone like this man, who visited San Francisco not too often. I didn't want romantic love or a permanent relationship. I didn't want anyone to replace Bob.

Later when I told a physician friend about my failure to find a sexual partner, she advised, "Don't ask for sex. Ask for hugs. Men your age are as afraid of sex as you are, and you may get some crazy responses if you come on too strong. Ask for caresses, and if the man agrees, you can tell in a few minutes what you both really want." That made sense. I'd been seeing too many movies of precipitous seductions. If I asked again, I'd ask for hugs.

A cousin of mine, whom I hadn't really known since we were children, was marrying for the second time. I sent her a letter when her husband died, and she phoned a year later when she learned of Bob's death. After that we talked by phone several times. Now I called to congratulate her.

She laughed joyously, and her voice had no old lady quaver in it. She sounded like a teenager. "I never thought I'd be so lucky as to find two wonderful men in one lifetime." I didn't recall her being giddy forty-five years ago, when she married for the first time. In fact, my recollection was of two quite stolid, serious twenty-year-olds, who were working hard to do everything right. Now she giggled, telling me about their wedding plans and all the children and grandchildren, his and hers, who would attend. Perhaps in some ways marriage was easier at their age. They had money, they wouldn't need to work, and the children were grown and on their own. Their only commitments would be to each other. But either of them could die at any time.

I wondered how she had the courage to marry again. Her first husband died horribly, tortured to death by cancer. What if she had to watch another beloved man die? I was briefly sad for her, thinking how short a time they might have together. Then, as she bubbled on and on, I was envious.

I remembered the specialness of being coupled. Gay, lesbian, or straight, being coupled meant that someone wanted you more than anyone else in the world. You were cherished and loved in an exclusive partnership.

Of course I remembered. When I felt weak, Bob shared his strength. If I was hurt, he comforted me. When I was brave, he backed me up. If I was foolish, he was wise. When I was happy, he laughed with me. More important than anything else, I was special to him. I felt myself smiling into the telephone as I congratulated my cousin and wished her all possible happiness.

The next day I had lunch with married friends. She had to leave early to return to work, so she casually touched his shoulder and bent over to give him a quick kiss, lips to lips, before she hurried away. They were at ease with each other; nonclutching love partners who knew they would be together as long as they both lived.

I did believe this type of love could be achieved more than once in a lifetime, but I also knew that I didn't want it again. I was absolutely certain about this. Of course, the chances were that I'd have no choice. There were too many old women in this country and too few old men. But if the statistics were reversed, if there were a plenitude of old men, I'd still remain alone.

I spiraled into grief again, suffering as if my coupled state had been newly torn from me. I felt as if I were left without a coat in a bitterly cold world. I was uncoupled, alone. I experienced this pain when I wailed my way onto the plane to Costa Rica and again with my Academy family, when Irma Lee and Joen were my therapists.

I would not forget Bob's love. Last October a friend sang, "Time Heals Everything" in a musical, *Relationships: A Cabaret.* He said he'd included that song for me, because of the lyrics, "Tuesday, Thursday, autumn, winter, next year, some year...Time heals everything...but loving you."

I decided to visit an old buddy, a gay psychologist who was also grieving. He had lost friends, family members, and a lover, just as I had. The year before Bob's death, my father, my ex-husband, and my longtime friend Velma all died. I mourned them, but these losses were overwhelmed by my loss of Bob. This man was mourning all his losses.

We talked freely together, understanding each other in a way that most people couldn't. We'd been through similar experiences. He was a devoutly religious man, who had attained a quiet, profound acceptance of death, that I admired in him.

He planned to have me sleep on his waterbed, while he used the single bed in his guest room. At bedtime he turned on the national and local news, which was repetitively violent. We saw bodies from all parts of the world, starved, bloodied, and grotesque. Then the local police began describing a shoot-out between teenage gangs. I remembered my physician friend's words about asking for hugs and said, "Please turn off the TV and come to the waterbed with me. We both need cuddling."

We lay clothed in each other's arms, softly, nonsexually caressing each other. Though I began to feel a slight desire for sex, I was content with this form of closeness, and he was very clear that this was all he wanted. We hugged quietly for a long time, then got undressed and went outside to sit in his hot tub under a brilliantly white full moon. In the water, he gave me a foot massage and I returned the favor.

We decided to share the waterbed. He fell asleep first, while I listened peacefully to his light snores. I didn't cry for Bob, although the breathing, so close to me, reminded me of all the years before Bob grew too sick for us to be together in our bed. I moved very quietly toward my friend and fell asleep with one hand touching his back.

We slept together each night of my visit. Sometimes he held me softly, my face against his bare chest. Once, as we snuggled together, half asleep, I felt his unaroused maleness against me. I turned and we kissed each other drowsily, and that was all. My body was softening and felt internally younger. It wasn't sex I'd needed, so much as the warmth of tender, sweet contact. It was a lovely visit, and we planned to spend time together again in a year.

Dream: I am walking in the mountains and see a lake far below me. There are people, tiny little figures in bright swimming suits of yellow, green, and brilliant red bits of flashing color. The people are swimming, waving, diving from rocks into the blue, blue water. I hear their shouts and laughter. I decide to climb down to join them, when suddenly there is no longer a path, but only a small flat area, where I am standing, and a sheer cliff. The tiny swimmers continue their happy play, and I wish I were with them, but there is no way for me to climb down to the lake. Bob appears just above me, clear against the rock, as young as he was when we first met, as beautiful as he was then, and I am thrilled to see him.

A miniature creek begins to flow between my feet, making the ground slippery. I have to lie down quickly in the mud, to avoid sliding over the edge. I yell, "Help me, sweetheart."

He can't respond. I realize he's not really there, even though I see him. I'm terrified, and again try to tell him I need his help to stand up and get onto safe ground, but he becomes a shadow against the sky. I have a full-scale panic attack, and awaken as it floods through my body.

My first awake thought was that this panic attack was physically very similar to an orgasm. I'd experienced panic attacks before, but this was my first in many years. Amazed, I turned on the light, and wrote a detailed description of my dream and my physical reaction to it. I decided to discuss panic disorders with other therapists to find out whether there were scientific studies of the physical similarity between anxiety attacks and orgasm. Could sufferers of panic disorders be taught to translate their body's panic reactions into a physically pleasant sensation? Would patients believe me if I suggested that they could train their brains to enjoy such sensations? That would be a real breakthrough for such sufferers.

When I finished writing, I turned out the light and lay back in the darkness. I began to think about my dream. At first, I didn't try to analyze it or do anything at all to understand it. I simply enjoyed Bob's being in my dream. Then I acknowledged his inaccessibility. Even in my dream, I could not bring him to life. Whether I continued to lie on the slippery path, found a way to join the swimmers, or only watched them from a distance, Bob was not in my life. I was alone.

I was still enjoying unavailable men. There was no real difference between the unavailable men a year ago and those I'd recently brought into my life. I had put a dangerous cliff between me and the swimmers, and found panic instead of sex. So be it. I didn't know what I really wanted any more than I did a year ago, when I dreamed that I was saying no to dancing with other men. I began to understand that I chose men who would never agree to sexual encounters with me. I must not be ready for sex. And I certainly was not ready for love.

I hoped I could go on dreaming of Bob, even if the dreams turned to nightmares. Stubbornly, I continued to refuse to say good-bye to him.

Roar as a roaring storm,
Thunder and keep thundering, and snort
With Evil winds.
Your feet are filled with restlessness
...
On your harp of sighs
I hear your dirge.
—Enheduanna, "Inanna and Ishkur"

More Therapy

The time was coming when I'd have to consider seriously how to support myself. I was running out of money. I could begin phoning other therapists to announce my availability to do workshops in their cities; I could set up my own workshops in San Francisco; or I could find a cheaper way to live. I didn't want to do more workshops, and my friends, Conchita de Diego and Carlos Lopez, had offered me free housing in Spain. So I leased my apartment to a young woman from Japan and went to Spain for the summer, using a free plane ticket I received as a participant in the Evolution of Psychotherapy Conference in Germany at the end of the summer.

I lived for a month in their apartment in Valencia and then went on to their home on the southern coast of Spain, near Herradura. It was a wonderful and inexpensive summer. In Valencia I wandered about the medieval section and explored nearby villages. In Herradura I swam every morning in the Mediterranean, and then studied Spanish with an attractive young woman, who had just gotten her degree in Spanish literature and hadn't yet been successful in finding permanent work. We chattered about anything and everything, while in the background her mother sat listening proudly to her educated daughter.

I loved Spain and yet sometimes at night I'd wake up, dreamless but repeating to myself, "How much more time will I have to live without Bob?" I learned to answer, "No more than I choose." I no longer seriously wanted to die, so I wasn't concerned that I might commit suicide precipitously. I told myself, "Go ahead and mourn. It's all right to be heartbroken because Bob is dead and you are old and alone."

I was living entirely on my social security, which delighted me. As the author of *Not To Worry*, I had taught myself not to worry, especially about money. I'd never been interested in finances. Like many husbands, Bob had taken care of all that, leaving me free to be irresponsible whenever I chose. I knew I was fortunate to have the luxurious and inexpensive option of a summer in Spain. And I would soon be augmenting social security with money I would earn in Germany.

In August, I went to Hamburg to participate in the first Evolution of Psychotherapy Conference to be held in Europe. Over five thousand psychotherapists attended this conference, and I was one of the stars. The European therapists crowded into my therapy demonstrations by the hundreds, and I received standing ovations. Men and women rushed to the podium after each session to praise my work and ask me questions. I was excited and awed by their praise, and came home with enough money to see me through a few more months.

My summer had been beautiful, but I was beginning to admit to myself that I was not merely bereft—I was depressed. My traveling and teaching were a way of masking this fact. I needed therapy, but I wasn't willing to commit myself to long-term work with a local therapist. Throughout my professional life I taught brief therapy, and I wanted what I had given others.

At the American Academy of Psychotherapists' annual conference in New Orleans, fifteen months after my therapy with my AAP family, I asked Al Pesso if I could be the first client in his day-long workshop. It was a spur-of-the-moment decision. I had heard of his work and knew that he was considered an outstanding therapist. A friend described his method as a cross between a Greek chorus and psychodrama, with special emphasis on the body, and that description was intriguing.

After explaining his methods to the large audience of psychotherapists, he began with me. "I often work sitting on the floor, because when you sit on chairs, you limit your scope. Do you mind doing that?"

"Not at all." We sat together on the floor with the audience around us.

I began: "What I want...I'm very tight—in my shoulders and neck. That's the physical part. The other...I guess it's just plain...I'm lonely. An example...I decided to walk on Bourbon Street last night. David Hawkins went with me. I had a wonderful time. I was bouncy, happy. And as soon as I got back to my room...Whew." I began crying. "Basically, I'm lonely. Bob and I were always together." I added, "I ought to get over this. Bob's been dead a long time."

Pesso suggested that I choose participants to act as my internal critic, voice of truth, witness to my feelings, and contact person. The contact person was to hold me.

From the beginning I resisted the idea of a contact person. "I don't want one. That's my whole problem. There is no contact person in my life without Bob."

Pesso said he thought it important that "At some point you allow yourself this help," but we went on working without such a person. Pesso and the "Greek chorus" repeated many of my words and underlined my feelings for me. I began to trust the process and especially trusted Pesso. Probing more deeply, I found myself back in my family home, when I was five years old and very ill with rheumatic fever. I reported, "My parents were young and panicky, and they didn't know what to do. Neither did the doctor.

There were no antibiotics then." I explained that I screamed whenever anyone tried to touch me, because their touches hurt my inflamed joints.

"You need to let someone hold you now," Pesso said.

Again I resisted this suggestion, but finally I leaned back into the arms of the contact person. I spoke of overhearing the doctor whisper to my parents that I was dying. "I knew I could only die at night, because of that stupid 'Now I lay me down to sleep' prayer. So I did everything I could to stay awake all night. I slept in the daytime. I didn't tell anyone what I was doing. No one could have helped me anyway."

The contact person said, "If I had been your father back then, you could have told me how terrified you were about dying. I would have held you and comforted you."

I was stunned. I could have been helped when I was five years old. It shouldn't have been necessary for me to figure everything out by myself and to refuse all touch. I began to appreciate that. It hadn't been just my own pain that kept me from allowing others to touch and comfort me. Probably my parents, too, had been uncomfortable with touch, I decided, remembering that their infrequent touches had been awkward and uncertain. I told Pesso, "I've spent my life trying to be independent. I only let Bob in. He knew how to barge right through my resistance."

As the contact person continued to hold me, his touch was an antidote to my childhood opposition to dependency. At Pesso's suggestion, I chose someone from the audience to play the ideal mother, and the contact person became an ideal father. I worked on my relationship with both of my parents.

I believed that I was finished with this work, when my back suddenly began to hurt. "It's the way I'm leaning against you," I told the contact person.

Pesso said, "Don't sit up. Still lean on him. Otherwise, you'll be doing the work yourself again. Stay against him. And now with the pain you feel in your back, push against him as if to get rid of him. Push against him. Push against him with all your might. And make sounds. Louder."

I yelled and pushed as hard as I could, while the contact person supported me silently. I couldn't push him away. Then, amazingly, the pain was gone. My body felt soft and relaxed. "There's no more pain," I said. "I feel very peaceful."

"Stay where you are and take in the experience. Get a flavor of it. How your body would have felt back then. How the father and the mother would have felt to you back then."

I sensed the image of myself—an ill, hurting child surrounded by knowing, responsive parents. I formed a concept of parental sufficiency and gave myself the fantasy of capable figures who understood what to do. Parents who let me have the independence I was struggling for, but in a serene way. I gathered these presences into myself. "Yes. That's nice. Easy."

Both ideal parents said, "If we'd been your parents back then, things would have been easier for you."

Pesso said, "Now we are finished."

As is often true of therapy's effects, it wasn't until later that I recognized how much I had accomplished. After allowing myself to be held and comforted, I stopped clinging so desperately to Bob's memory.

Memories do not die
a sudden death
nor are they born
de novo all at once
but rise and fall a rolling wave
of feeling muted by time
Long long shall I remember you.
—William Kir-Stimon, "Of Memories"

Good-Bye

After my work with Al Pesso, I felt ready to say good-bye to Bob. I used the good-bye formula Fritz Perls created and that Bob and I expanded on later:

> *Review the years with the loved one, and stop at any scene that doesn't feel finished. In fantasy, enter the scene and complete it.*
>
> *Create a final scene. Express your resentments and all the negative feelings you still carry, plus any unfulfilled wishes or hopes, and let these go. Voice your appreciations.*
>
> *Say good-bye. Imagine yourself at the scene of the funeral or burial, and state, "You are dead," and "Good-bye." These words form a powerful acknowledgment that the dead person is no longer present in this world.*

To *Review* my lifetime with Bob, I started by opening the photo album I put together after his death. The first photo was of Bob, age forty-eight, taken the year we became lovers. He was handsome, strong, and smiling. I studied the photo carefully and then put it down.

I imagined him with me in my office in Salinas, our office in Carmel, the workshop house we rented in the middle '60s in Menlo Park. "You were my teacher, my therapist, my love. You changed my life."

Next I remembered a secret place where we sometimes went to be together. There were squirrels and tall pines, a hidden bench, and a beautiful view of Monterey Bay. I imagined the two of us sitting again on that bench. I was struck by the fact that we were so much younger than we knew then. There was nothing unfinished and nothing new I wanted to tell him. "I am enjoying this place one last time with you." I imagined that he said, "I love you, baby," and I answered, "I love you, too. For always."

I looked at the photos of our wedding day. We were on the lawn at Western Institute, standing in a circle with our friends and grown children. My daughter Claudia played the flute, while a friend sang in his deep, baritone voice. We told each other of our love, and a minister friend married us. There was nothing unfinished in that lovely memory.

Putting down the album, I remembered us working together in a resort in Japan, where rhododendron bloomed in fantastic colors and Mt. Fuji shone in the distance. I saw us in England, unable to stop giggling in a very sedate restaurant where the British diners, unlike us, knew how to use their knives and forks without making a sound. I saw us in Paris; in Israel; in Italy with the video cameras whirring; in a farmhouse in Germany where fresh bread was baked every morning just below our bedroom; in Australia and New Zealand and Canada; in so many different cities and countries. I heard us talking theory, building on each other's ideas, figuring out how to minimize transference by encouraging clients to create their own scenes and act them out to redecide key issues in their lives. I remembered writing together, doing therapy together, and being the famous "Goulding team." I saw us together at the International Transactional Analysis Association Conference when we received the Eric Berne Memorial Award, and at the first Evolution of Psychotherapy Conference.

These memories became unbearably painful. I didn't want to say good-bye to our work together. Before Bob was too sick to travel, I was the one begging to retire early to have fun, be lazy, and just enjoy ourselves. Now I yearned for us to be cotherapists again.

I sat in my bedroom weeping for a long time, and then went to the swimming pool below my apartment. I swam slowly, not counting laps, just crying into the water. Never, never again would we be cotherapists. We'd never again ask the participants, "Who's first?" or "What do you want to change for yourself today?" I'd never hear his loud "Aha!" when someone made an important self-discovery. We wouldn't hear ourselves say the same thing at the same time—which we often did because we thought alike—and then start laughing together. I wouldn't see the stiff, silly bow that he sometimes gave, when people praised him or applauded. Those were exciting years, so full of liveliness and humor and skill.

I swam and cried, and finally in the water, I said good-bye to our work together. Then because I didn't know what else to do, I got dressed and walked the city streets.

The next morning and afternoon, I ignored my good-byes, but in the evening I began again. I went quickly through many occasions—births of grandchildren, holidays, travel—and I didn't get stuck on any of them. I finished the Review.

The next part of my good-bye was to *Create* a final scene. I imagined Bob comatose in his hospital bed in our study, before I got into his bed for the final time. The oxygen tube was in place, his skin was pink and soft, and he couldn't hear me at all. It was almost the end. I began, as we had taught others to do. "I'm saying good-bye to you, my dearest love. You didn't want to die. You loved life. You had been so extravagantly exuberant for many years."

I heard myself, as my own therapist, saying gently, "Tell about you, not about him. This is for your benefit, not his." That is what I might be saying to a client.

I didn't like my therapist intrusion, and told that part of me, "I can take as long as I please, so be quiet." Then to a comatose Bob, "You held out against death with fantastic arrogance, day after day. I resent that we didn't say good-bye. But if you'd allowed us to say good-bye to each other, that would have been like giving up. In spite of your terrible pain, you didn't give up."

I remembered that a friend, who traveled across the country to visit Bob before he died, later told me, "All I wanted was for us to hold each other and cry and cry because we'd never see each other again, but Bob wouldn't permit it. He said, 'Don't cry. I'm not dead yet.'"

Then came the terrible days of pain and near-blindness and deafness, and Bob said, "I want to die. I want to go to sleep and not wake up." And still we said no good-byes.

"I admired your courage, and grieved silently for your unbearable distress. I resent that we, who'd always before been so open with each other, stayed silent at the end. The truth is, I would have mourned you just as long, just as sadly, no matter what you and I said to each other during those last, terrible days. And now I am letting you go."

I looked for other resentments. "I'm done with my anger over your alcohol and cigarettes. I have no leftover resentments there."

Other resentments? "Such piddling ones—your high-handed bossiness, which was just like mine. We were two bossy people."

I imagined him saying what he often said, "We're both oldest children, so of course we fight. What's the difference? We keep right on loving." Yes, my sweet, that was true. No resentments left, only an apology.

"I wish I'd argued less with you. Through all our years together, we argued over who was right, whose facts were most correct, and who had a corner on the truth. I often kept a fight going when there was no ultimate truth involved, only differences of opinion. Oh, my love, our issues were trivial. You knew that always. I know that now." I wished that I could do that part over, be nicer, more conciliatory, but I knew I probably wouldn't change even if there were a second chance.

Unfulfilled wishes, hopes, or dreams? "You wanted to see Ireland and I wanted to see Scotland, and we had planned to visit both countries together. Then you couldn't do it. That was a wish we deferred too long. Now I'll probably take Claudia to see Scotland without you."

I shut my eyes and searched my memory for anything important I'd omitted. "I resent that you died, that you aren't here with me this minute." Resentments couldn't bring Bob back any more than sorrow could.

Other resentments? I didn't think so. Sadness, of course, for both of us. "I am sad and lonely without you, and I am sad that you are missing these years. I am sad that you are not alive to know that you have two new grandchildren, a boy and a girl."

And my appreciations. "I appreciate your intelligence, your power, your zest, your creativity, your beautiful caring, and your faithfulness. In every way you were faithful. You always accepted me. I didn't have to prove anything to be loved by you. Your love was unconditional and enduring, as was mine for you. I have had such a difficult time existing without your love. The gift you gave me, the most important gift of all, was your love. Thank you."

Then I said *Good-Bye.* I did not imagine the sunny day we buried Bob's ashes, but rather a fierce winter afternoon with cold, driving rain and soaking earth. My grief demanded such weather. I imagined that I was at our institute beside the redwood tree. I held the wooden box of ashes in my hands, mildewed but still intact. The hole in the ground was ready in front of me. I opened the box, unsealed the plastic liner, and felt the powdery ash and the few nuggets big enough to be pieces of bone. I poured them slowly into the open hole, and watched them merge with water and wet earth. The cold rain washed my hands clean of ashes. I used our old shovel to fill the hole, and then tamped down the dirt. "Good-bye, my dearest Bob."

In my imagination, I walked away over the mountain and north through the valley into San Francisco. The next week I finally ordered a stone to be put over the ashes. It said simply, Robert L. Goulding, MD, 1917–1992.

It may be, that the loosened soul may find
Some new delight of living without limbs,
Bodiless joy of flesh-untrammeled mind,
Peace like a sky where starlike spirit swims.
It may be, that the million cells of sense,
Loosed from their seventy years' adhesion, pass
Each to some joy of changed experience,
Weight in the earth or glory in the grass;
It may be that we cease; we cannot tell.
Even if we cease life is a miracle.
—John Masefield, "Sonnets"

And Then

When I helped patients say good-bye to loved ones who had died, they usually reported a brief increase in mourning, followed by a profound peacefulness, as if an internal weight was lifted from them. I felt this also, and yet I was still depressed. As I had predicted, my dreams of Bob ceased, and I was sad about that. Then I had another dream.

> *Dream: Bob is being brought toward me by a nurse. He's thin, taller than I remembered, and expressionless. Although he walks unaided with a nurse beside him, he doesn't seem to be alive. I am not surprised by this and react as if that is how he naturally would be. I rush up to him and tell the nurse to leave us alone. I plan that Bob and I will spend the day doing things he always liked. I tell him this, but it is obvious that he can't hear or respond. I decide that doesn't*

matter. "We'll have fun together." I suggest a 49ers game, saying, "I know you'll like that." There is no response. Finally I admit, "I really can't please you, because you don't exist." He vanishes.

Waking, I decided this was the saddest dream I had ever had, but I accepted it without tears. The dream told the truth and was perhaps necessary following my good-bye. Bob did not exist. I would remember him always with great love, but even dreams could not bring us together again.

I received an offer for the Western Institute property and agreed to sell it for half of what it was worth. I was disappointed at the amount, but I was free. Escrow closed. The part of my life that included Bob and Western Institute was now decisively over.

I went on another trip, this time to the International Transactional Analysis Conference in Aruba, where I was with old friends from all over the world. I actually dared to give a workshop, including therapy and discussion in Spanish. Before starting I said in Spanish, "There are two options. I can speak in English with translation into Spanish, or I can speak in Spanish with translation into good Spanish." They insisted that I continue in Spanish, and I rarely needed help. I was so pleased with myself that I told the audience I would return to Costa Rica after the winter holidays to study a few more weeks with Carlos, and then I'd do another workshop in Spanish during the August conference in San Francisco.

At the final banquet, the band played "Happy Birthday" for someone. It was October 29, Bob's birthday too. I had remembered, of course, but had ignored the date until I heard the music. I felt again the old, sharp, physical ache, as from an abdominal surgery that had not healed. I left the banquet and went to bed early, skipping the party and the trip to the casinos.

The next day a group of us sailed on a large catamaran to a fine snorkeling site, and I laughed more than anyone else, swam, and even drank rum in my diet colas. I felt ridiculously young and joyous. If this was what we criticized as lability in my student days, I would make the most of it. I preferred wild mood swings to being stuck in what I now realized was a chronic depression. I returned to San Francisco.

I had denied being depressed by telling myself I was bereft, but now I realized that I'd been depressed for at least five years, since Bob became seriously ill. I felt the heaviness even when I laughed the loudest.

I could write a book on depression. Depression: bereft. Depression: emptiness. Depression: anger turned inward. Post-traumatic depression, chronic depression, underlying depression. Depression programmed from childhood and reinstated or exacerbated by loss, by memories, by almost anything.

Depression: passive, a greyness and apathy, when nothing was worth experiencing. I fought this passive depression by focusing outside myself on exciting places, workshop clients, family, and friends. I could be proud of that fight, though I wasn't.

Depression: active, self-induced. Although I thought I had finished with my guilt, I still felt guilty. I continued to overwhelm myself with irrational guilt for my actions, when I had been truly overwhelmed with the burden of Bob's dying. I hadn't done enough for him, and what I had done was wrong. I was manufacturing emotional bile and pushing it through every available crack of my psyche. I could not seem to fight myself, the self-poisoner.

Depression was life without Bob. I lost my heart when I lost Bob. He had cared for me and loved away my hard-core, pre-Bob depression. Without Bob, trying to love myself was an absurdity.

It was almost two years since I had written: "Sometimes I tried to comfort myself by imagining that I was talking with Erving Polster. He phoned often after Bob's death and was especially compassionate. I fantasized flying to La Jolla to tell him, 'I can't go on like this.' I'd tell him how much I hurt. The fantasy was briefly comforting, but I didn't act on it."

From my session with Al Pesso, I knew how strongly I believed that I needed to sit up and take care of myself. Now I decided to give myself what I had wanted. I phoned Erv and flew to La Jolla to see him.

The work we did together was exactly what I needed. It was amazing, almost magical. With his help, I banished the guilt that had never been reasonable, and afterward I played with Miriam Polster's collection of kaleidoscopes and spent time with both of them. I felt cherished by Erving and Miriam, and took their love home with me. Though I was still depressed, I now believed that I could get out from under it.

Erv gave me the manuscript for his newest book, *A Population of Selves,* and when I got home I bought a kaleidoscope. I canceled my appointments and hid away from everyone, working hour after hour to cure myself. I studied Erv's book, relearned gestalt vocabulary and theory, and applied Erv's ideas to me.

Bob, Erv, Miriam, and I used to make presentations at the same conferences, sometimes on the same panels, and we were approximately the same age. We were peers and friends. Now, as I worked on myself, I used Erv and Miriam as models for the competent, caring parents I needed. In the past, many people wrote to Bob and me to tell us how they used our books, *Changing Lives* or *Not to Worry,* to change their own lives. I couldn't use our books to cure myself because I wrote them. I knew them too well. Having to struggle to understand and apply *A Population of Selves* made cure possible.

Many people have the mistaken belief that change and cure occur spontaneously during therapy, without effort; that the right memory, the right insight, especially the right interpretation will bring startling and instantaneous peace or power or whatever the client is seeking. Humans are not computers and cannot be reprogrammed easily. Even with splendid help, we have to do a lot of the work ourselves. So now I was sitting up and taking care of me, knowing that I could get more help whenever necessary.

First I had to keep myself from bringing back my guilt. I held on tightly to my memory of the session in La Jolla, of the loving, appreciative, understanding words I had heard from Erv. I'd catch myself fighting those words, insisting, "If he really knew me, or if I had told him about this rather than that, he'd have known how rotten I was." I even tried to make myself believe "He never did like me, he was just being therapeutic." I had to remind myself, over and over, that in his book he wrote about his work with a patient: "Everything I say to him is as close to the truth as I can get it." I had to believe in his truthfulness. I fought hard to maintain that belief against the garbage I was hurling at it.

The therapy I experienced since Bob's death was profoundly important to me. The sessions with my American Academy of Psychotherapy family may have saved my life. Don St. John helped me break through the wall I'd erected against knowing my anger at Bob. The women's group made me somehow softer, easier, and opened the door for me to be in touch with healing women. Al Pesso showed me how much I needed support, and he gave me an important sample of that support. And now Erv had given me a magic love and helped me banish guilt. All of this was beautiful and invaluable, and I had to take the next, giant step.

I'd used the love from these therapists as substitutes for Bob's love. As long as I'd had Bob, I hadn't had to love myself. His active, noisy, vibrant, wholehearted love had been enough. It was Bob and not I who had loved me. Without him, the depression I'd experienced since childhood had returned and grown more virulent. If I accepted other therapists as substitute love-givers, I would need them as I had needed Bob—forever.

Self-therapy wasn't easy. In fact, I was one of the most difficult patients I had ever had. As fast as I found success, I crossed it out or, as Erv had written in his book, "scribbled over it."

I studied Erv's descriptions of the various Selves within each person. I could brighten my life by liking my Selves, but there were so many that I despised. I tried first to identify the Selves I liked: my creative, intelligent, adventuresome Selves; my caring Self. But I had no energy for this. My energy was focused on the negative, so I started there.

First was the unpopular Self with the stringy hair, who was disliked in first grade and then skipped from first to third grade to face a roomful of eight-year-olds who really hated her. She was ugly and always flunked popularity, femininity, and grace. As an adult, I still hesitated and stiffened before entering a room where people had already gathered. Letting the past intrude into the present, I continued to fear the imagined contempt of a group.

There were worse Selves than "Stringy Hair." There was the bossy, arrogant Self who guarded Stringy Hair by pretending great self-confidence. She shouted out answers ahead of the other kids, argued incessantly, and was almost always right. She talked too much, then and now, especially at election time.

I attacked these Selves derisively, and then realized that this self-derisive Self was my real enemy. She was an exaggeration of the way the eight-year-olds had treated me.

I worked from page one of *A Population of Selves* to the end; free-associating, struggling, and writing down whatever I needed to remember. Each time I became stuck or discouraged, I reached for my kaleidoscope and focused on its lovely colors. Then I went back to work. I had thought I would have to change all the hated parts of me, and made some attempts to do this. But I discovered that merely recognizing and accepting these Selves without derision diminished their importance. I could live with them. All of them. I accepted my self-derisive Self, now that I understood where she came from. This mere acceptance calmed her down.

I had taught hundreds of therapists to love themselves, insisting that change cannot occur without self-love. The therapists who studied with Bob and me might be shocked to learn that I had lacked self-love. Surrounded by Bob's love, I remained unaware of my need to learn to love myself. Well, I could whine about learning late or be very happy with what I was now achieving. I chose happiness.

Eight days after I began my self-therapy, I woke in the morning without depression. It was like awakening in childhood after a long period of fever and knowing absolutely that the fever was gone. I'd made it! I wrote a thank-you letter to Erv, and we talked by phone. I phoned friends, many of whom had not even known that I was depressed, to tell them, "I'm OK now!"

My son and daughters had been my allies, my treasures, tender and fun and enriching. Together and separately, they kept me going through the bad times. Now I could tell them too, "I'm OK!"

and "Thank you for everything."

I phoned a friend on the East Coast, who was away, and had a beautiful conversation with his lover, a man I scarcely knew. When I asked him to relay the message that I'd stopped being depressed, we talked for a long time about the brightness and goodness of life without depression, and neither of us felt compelled to be therapist for the other.

During the next few months, I was dazzled by my discoveries about myself. I seemed to be opening wide doors into new sunlight, and each door led to new doors. During an AAP panel on The Person of the Psychotherapist, I spoke introspectively about my life since Bob's death, and afterward people came up to me lovingly. I made appropriate responses to them, smiled, hugged, and took in almost nothing that they said. As I hurried from the podium to my room, I had only a vague awareness that people were reaching out to me with love. Afterward, I didn't remember who any of them were. This had been my pattern for years: I took in applause for my work, but not loving statements, and in this way maintained the fiction that I was still the awkward, unpopular kid in grade school. No wonder I was often lonely.

I worked on this with my AAP family, and during the rest of the conference I sought out new people, to appreciate them and connect with them. And I believed the loving comments they gave me.

I even danced! When a man in my AAP family asked why I had refused to dance with him the night before, I ran down a list of reasons, which he didn't accept: "I don't dance; I can't dance because I never learned how; I can't hear music well; maybe I'm phobic," and then explained, "I am ashamed to let anyone see how gawky and inept I am." After admitting this, I agreed to go dancing that evening with him and his wife.

In a panic I phoned my daughter Karen, who dances, to ask her advice. She knew I couldn't dance and told me just to dance freestyle. She said, "Listen to the music and move your body however you want to. You don't have to follow. You don't even have to move much. Just enjoy."

That was what I did, for more than three hours. I amazed myself.

> *Dream: Bob and I are in bed, not cuddling but holding hands as we chat pleasantly. After a while he says, "I'm tired as hell. I need to sleep."*

When the dream ended, I felt nostalgia rather than pain. He'd said exactly this in reality many times. In the following weeks, I had more dreams of Bob that were sweet, ordinary, and peaceful. It was what I had wanted so desperately before. Now that my depression was gone, I enjoyed these happy stories I invented or remembered while asleep. I still missed Bob. Occasionally I awakened at night crying, but I could cry and feel light at the same time, lighter than in years.

I flew to Mexico to colead with Muriel James the last two workshops in my professional life. I would be seventy within a month and was eager to retire. I would continue to present Redecision therapy at conferences around the world, but would not treat patients or run workshops.

Returning from Mexico, I wheeled my suitcase into my apartment, and through my windows I saw a grey, silky fog and clouds heavy with more rain. Then the clouds shifted, allowing the sun to spotlight three bright red geraniums in the pot on my balcony. I'd bought the plant before leaving San Francisco. Now I was an old lady with geraniums. The flowers trembled in a slight breeze and seemed to be waving hello. I was home. Had I ever called this home before? I didn't think so.

It rained all night, and the next morning I awoke to the fantastic brightness of the sea and city after rain. Such total beauty everywhere! I lay in bed, looking out at the still wet, shining rooftops; the cargo ships, tankers, and sailboats; the puffed-out clouds. There was nothing at all that I had to do.

I realized that I was now in the fourth and final stage of my life. I'd had my growing-up years, then the years of my first marriage and the growing up of my children, then my years with Bob. Like the other stages, Bob's and my time together had been a whole, with a beginning and an end. I was now in a new and interesting era.

I moved to a two-bedroom apartment with the same grand view. I gave away almost all the furniture that belonged to Bob and me, except the lovely cabinet we purchased together, and redecorated. My living room was now mostly white, with bright Moroccan rugs. I had a home that reflected my tastes, and I could entertain overnight guests easily.

I planned to continue traveling. I scheduled scuba lessons in Honduras. There were exciting places I had not yet visited, above and below the sea.

I didn't want to be in love again. I was choosing to be alone, because I didn't want the constrictions of couplehood. I preferred the challenge and sweetness of nonsexual intimacy with many different people. I wanted to care for myself.

I was learning to be a loving, intelligent, and powerful parent to myself, and began to test the concept of internal peace, something quite new for me. I talked often with Irma Shepherd, Joen Fagan, Bernice Turoff, and other psychotherapists from the women's workshop and strengthened my friendships with women. I knew that I could get help from colleagues whenever I needed it.

Even though I now had red geraniums, I decided to stop calling myself an old lady; I no longer felt old. Months passed, and I realized that I was happy most of the time.

When I began keeping the journal that became this book, I titled it "Widowed" because I thought that was all I was or would be. Through the struggle of the past three-and-a-half years, I mourned, at my own speed, the death of my lover, Bob. The love between myself and my family and friends helped me through this period. I also sustained myself with my love of the world—the little red frogs and howler monkeys, the beautiful temples of India and Angkor Wat—and my love for San Francisco, my favorite city in this world. As my mourning eased, I had to learn to love myself as well. With this accomplished, I no longer defined myself solely by what I lost. I had been widowed, but that was not my identity.

I am a woman for whom life is an adventure, and also a miracle of loving and being loved.

Acknowledgments

I want to thank my colleagues who functioned as personal therapists for me when I needed them: My AAP family; the participants in the women's workshop at Isla Mujeres; Al Pesso, Pesso Boyden System Psychomotor, Franklin, New Hampshire; Don St. John, MA, Seattle, Washington; and Erving Polster, PhD, La Jolla, California.

Many people gave me their love and support while I was writing this book. I especially want to thank my son and daughters, David Edwards, Karen Edwards, and Claudia Pagano; my sisters, Bette Kreger, Laurie Barrett, Margaret Beagle, and Diane Jones; and my friends Ruth McClendon, Les Kadis, Reiko True, Muriel James, Joen Fagan, Irma Lee Shepherd, David Hawkins, Neal Blumenfeld, Bernice Turoff, Michiko Fukazawa, Jorge Ortiz, Conchita de Diego, Carlos Lopez, Kozo Rokkaku, Jeff Zeig, Felipe Garcia, Barbara Hibner, June Brevdy, and Joan Minninger.

All of you live in my heart.

About the Author

MARY MCCLURE GOULDING, MSW, is a well-known psychotherapist and teacher. She and her late husband, Robert L. Goulding, MD, developed Redecision therapy, a system of brief therapy that is widely used by psychotherapists in many countries. She has lectured and given workshops all over the world. She is one of three women and the only social worker to be honored as a major presenter at all of the Evolution of Psychotherapy conferences, 1985, 1990, and 1995, and at the first European Evolution of Psychotherapy conference in Hamburg, Germany, 1994. She and Bob Goulding wrote three books: *Changing Lives Through Redecision Therapy, The Power Is in the Patient*, and *Not to Worry.* She wrote a biography of Dr. Goulding, *Sweet Love Remembered.* She is retired and lives in San Francisco.

Papier-Mache Press

At Papier-Mache Press, it is our goal to identify and successfully present important social issues through enduring works of beauty, grace, and strength. Through our work we hope to encourage empathy and respect among diverse communities, creating a bridge of understanding between the mainstream audience and those who might not otherwise be heard.

We appreciate you, our customer, and strive to earn your continued support. We also value the role of the bookseller in achieving our goals. We are especially grateful to the many independent booksellers whose presence ensures a continuing diversity of opinion, information, and literature in our communities. We encourage you to support these bookstores with your patronage.

We publish many fine books about women's experiences. We also produce lovely posters and T-shirts that complement our anthologies. Please ask your local bookstore which Papier-Mache items they carry. To receive our complete catalog, send your request to Papier-Mache Press, 135 Aviation Way, #14, Watsonville, CA 95076, or call our toll-free number, 800-927-5913.

More Papier-Mache Press Titles of Related Interest

If I Had My Life to Live Over I Would Pick More Daisies
Edited by Sandra Haldeman Martz

The companion volume to the wildly popular *When I Am an Old Woman I Shall Wear Purple,* this anthology focuses on the decisions, public and private, that shape women's lives. Inspired by the title poem in which an older woman looks back on a life sensibly lived and wishes she had "eaten more ice cream and less beans," editor Sandra Martz has brought together stories, poems, and photographs that "cut across a spectrum of age, race, and ways of life." *(Kirkus Reviews)*

ISBN 0-918949-24-6, trade paper
ISBN 0-918949-25-4, hardcover

Learning to Sit in the Silence: A Journal of Caretaking
Elaine Marcus Starkman

Writer and teacher Elaine Marcus Starkman addresses the issue of caring for aging relatives in this moving book. Based on her experiences caring for her aging mother-in-law over a ten-year period, *Learning to Sit in the Silence* reveals in journal form the day-to-day joys and challenges of caregiving.

"*...for everyone who loves life and recognizes that caregiving takes strength, fortitude, compassion, and a whole lot of love.*"—Phyllis J. Lessin, Asst. Chief, Alzheimer's Disease Research Center, UC San Diego

ISBN 0-918949-43-2, trade paper
ISBN 0-918949-44-0, hardcover

Washing the Stones: Selected Poems 1975–1995
Maude Meehan

A well-respected activist and California poet, seventy-five-year-old Maude Meehan speaks eloquently for her generation. Her clear voice empowers women who read this poetic memoir of passion, love, and politics. Chronicling one woman's journey, Meehan's rich observations commemorate the experiences of a life lived fully, with her partner of fifty-seven years, and after his death.

"*These poems celebrate family, children, and long years of sensual love. The exemplary title poem, "Washing the Stones," particularly speaks of loss and continuity. There are many lovely poems in this collection.*"—Grace Paley, author of *The Collected Stories*

ISBN 0-918949-85-8, trade paper